MW01026354

Just Beneath

the

SURFACE

M. SHAY HOLMES

ISBN 978-1-68570-489-6 (paperback)
ISBN 978-1-68570-490-2 (digital)

Copyright © 2022 by M. Shay Holmes

All rights reserved. No part of this publication may be reproduced, distributed, or transmitted in any form or by any means, including photocopying, recording, or other electronic or mechanical methods without the prior written permission of the publisher. For permission requests, solicit the publisher via the address below.

Christian Faith Publishing
832 Park Avenue
Meadville, PA 16335
www.christianfaithpublishing.com

Printed in the United States of America

I would like to extend a special thanks to my husband, Dean. His knowledge of history and the Bible, as well as his passion to continuously study and learn more, has made him a great source of information and a great encourager. His research and wisdom have been invaluable. Also, to my kids, who are the original reason I began to write the book, so that they might have some of their dad's research in print, as well as my own.

CONTENTS

CHAPTER 1

Introduction

The continuity of the Bible from Genesis to Revelation is one of the profound confirmations that the Scriptures are the inerrant and inspired Word of God. The division between the Old and New Testaments is best understood not as two separate readings or that the New Testament is newer and more modern and, therefore, relevant Word but rather as a difference in focus while continuing an intricate saga. The Bible is like a huge jigsaw puzzle, and we begin our Christian walk a little overwhelmed by so many loose and apparently unconnected pieces. But just like working our puzzle—if we are willing to continue to sort colors, shapes, and sizes and continue to connect our puzzle, one piece at a time—eventually, we'll begin to see a picture. Gradually, over time, it becomes easier to find the pieces and becomes more apparent where they go.

The New Testament is concealed in the Old Testament. The Old Testament is revealed in the New Testament. God fulfills his Word in the New Testament; he does not do away with it. I have heard many Christians say that they don't read the Old Testament because the New Testament is the more important Word. Well, brother, if you refuse to work on any of the blue pieces of your puzzle, you will still make some slow progress on *parts* of the picture, but you'll never get anywhere close to seeing the *whole* picture. The Old and New Testaments work together to create a complete image of Christ. And yes, Christ and the message of grace are all over the Old Testament.

The Old and New Testaments also work together in an intricate and intentional manner that reveals the sovereignty of God and his constant intervention and caring in the lives of mankind.

The apparent "contradictions" found between the two parts of the Bible, when studied in more depth, turn out to be a divine balance. The focus of the Old Testament is God's judgment and his need for justice. This is an important facet of God. After all, the understanding of the Law is what points us to the need for Christ. If we don't understand God's standard, how can we know if we are capable of upholding it? And if we could uphold the stringent standards of God, we wouldn't need Christ. Throughout the Old Testament, we see the Law, the rules, the harsh punishments and a theme of vengeance. This is indicative of God's standard and his justice. God hates sin, and it must be punished. His sense of fairness can allow for no less than his absolute justice. Though the focus of the Old Testament is justice, it is heavily intertwined with the story of God's mercy and grace. All you have to do is look beneath the surface.

The core of the New Testament is God's grace and mercy—another important aspect of His personality. His justice, however, and his standards remain unchanged. Through God's mercy and grace, he sent his Son to pay the penalty for our sin so that his sense of justice would be satisfied—a son who met God's standard. What a fabulous demonstration of the perfect balance and perfect mercy. God says there must be a punishment to create perfect justice then offers himself to receive the punishment in a show of perfect mercy. We cannot separate God into different compartments based on man's definitions nor can we separate the Old and New Testaments. God is not only grace and love, and He is not only vengeance and justice. For without his need for justice, there would be no need for his mercy and grace. Without his mercy and grace, it's not possible to meet the standard he requires, and his sense of justice would require him to destroy us.

The connections between the Old Testament and the New weave together like a beautiful and colorful tapestry that shines with the glory of God. The colors are vibrant, explosive, and available for all to see. All we have to do is look beneath the surface. A primary example of this intricate connectedness is the genealogies of the Bible. When we study this in more depth, however, we see that nothing is in the Scriptures without purpose.

Within the Jewish culture, the names of their children had meanings. This was important to the Jews, for they were often prophetic of their children's lives or related to events that occurred at their birth. Often, we think that because God gave man free will, he doesn't interfere in our lives; he simply has foreknowledge of our future decisions. We don't recognize the purpose of the Bible. It is not just a history of the Jewish people or a book of interesting stories. It's God's Word, written for us, with the specific purpose of pointing us toward Christ. Old and New Testaments alike point directly to Christ. The events of people's lives are orchestrated for that purpose. God wanted them, and us, and all of those in between to see His hand at work. We see this in the names of Noah's genealogy. It starts with Adam, whose name means "man." Adam begot Seth whose name means "appointed." Of course, Adam named his son appointed because he was appointed as a replacement for Abel after Cain killed him. God, however, had another plan in mind. Seth begot Enos, meaning "mortal." Enos begot Cainan, aka "sorrow." The next in line was Mahalalel, meaning "the blessed God." Mahalalel begot Jared whose name means "shall come down" and then there was Enoch, which means "teaching." His son was Methuselah whose life was a sign of God's grace. His name means "his death shall bring," and sure enough, his death brought the flood. God extended Methuselah's life longer than anyone's, 969 years, thus giving the people in Noah's day the longest opportunity possible in which to repent. Methuselah begot Lamech, meaning "despairing," who then begot Noah, which means "rest."

If we take their names in order, Adam, Seth, Enos, Cainan, Mahalalel, Jared, Enoch, Methuselah, Lamech, Noah, and then we substitute the meanings for their names, we get a profound prophecy of Christ all the way back in Genesis chapter 5: *Man appointed mortal sorrow. The blessed God shall come down teaching. His death shall bring the despairing rest.* Here, we have the fall of man and Christ's birth and death leading to our salvation—all written thousands of years before our Lord and all in the names of men. Though these men had free will in naming their sons, God was creating a model of his coming Son.

Another great example of the hidden meanings within the genealogies of the Scripture is the genealogy of our Lord. We have four gospels telling us of the life of Christ. The genealogies appear to contradict one another, but in actuality, when we search beneath the surface of the Scriptures, we find a fabulous balance and complete consistency. But we must use the Old Testament to understand why this apparent "inconsistency" exists.

First, in the book of Matthew, we see Christ's genealogy through Joseph, the husband of Mary. Matthew was a Jew and presents Jesus as a king and from the perspective of a Jewish man. He begins with Abraham, the beginning of the Jews, goes through David and then Solomon and continues on through Jechoniah and, eventually, Matthew 1:16 says, "And Jacob begat Joseph the husband of Mary, of whom was born Jesus, who is called Christ." This genealogy grants Christ the legal right to the throne. The kingship is inherited through the man. Jesus is not a blood relative of Joseph, of course, but is a legal son.

The book of Mark has no genealogy, but he presents Christ as a servant, and the Jews did not keep pedigrees on their servants, so a lack of a genealogy is consistent.

The apparent contradiction of genealogies is between the book of Matthew and the book of Luke. Luke presents Christ as a man. Luke is a gentile and a doctor and takes the genealogy of Christ through the literal bloodline. Being a gentile, he doesn't take it from Abraham but rather all the way back to Adam. If you follow Christ's genealogy in the book of Luke, it continues through to David, and then instead of Solomon, it goes through Nathan, another son of David. It names the father of Joseph as Heli. The genealogy works its way backward and actually starts with Jesus and ends with Adam, so Luke 3:23 says, "And Jesus himself began to be about thirty years of age, being (as it was supposed) the son of Joseph, which was the son of Heli." What? I thought that Joseph was the son of Jacob, according to Matthew. This appears to contradict, and if I believe the Bible to be without error, they can't both be true, can they?

It just so happens that they are both indeed true. You will notice that in Luke, it says, "As it was supposed." You see, Heli wasn't the father of Joseph, he was the father-in-law. Luke is giving the genealogy of Jesus through his bloodline, through Mary. Women are rarely mentioned in genealogies, and Jesus did inherit the right to the kingdom and the land that Heli had through Mary because she had no brothers. For a full understanding of what is happening here, we have to go back to Numbers chapters 26 and 27. In Numbers 26:33, we are introduced briefly to a man named Zelophehad. It is said that Zelophehad had only daughters and no sons. Later in chapter 27:1–11, we see the daughters of Zelophehad approach Moses with a petition. They complain to Moses that their father has died in the wilderness but has no sons to inherit. If he had no one to inherit his land, then his name simply disappeared into their history. The daughters petitioned Moses for a solution. Moses went to the Lord, and the Lord told Moses to allow daughters to inherit in the event that the father had no sons. So what would happen is that the daughters would marry and then inherit in their husbands name, with the husband "as was supposed" the son of the wife's father. Well, thousands of years later, this has huge implications. Jesus was not the blood relative of Joseph, but he was the blood relative of Mary. The genealogy of Jesus in the book of Luke is actually the genealogy of Mary. Mary's father had no sons, only daughters. So like Zelophehad's daughters, Mary inherited her father's inheritance through the name of her husband, and Jesus, therefore, inherited the right to the throne, not only through the legal line of Joseph but also through the bloodline of his mother. He would not have inherited this right if his mother had brothers because they would have inherited it instead. In addition to that, had Mary not married within her own tribe, then according to Numbers 36, she couldn't then inherit in her tribe. But this wasn't a problem for Christ because Joseph was of the same tribe—the tribe of Judah.

There is one other important thing to point out regarding the importance of Christ's inheritance through Mary. This line allows

Christ to avoid the curse of Jechoniah. God cursed Jechoniah, the Old Testament version of his name is Coniah, in Jeremiah 22:28–30. He cursed him and stated that, "No man of his seed shall prosper, sitting upon the throne of David, and ruling any more in Judah." Satan must have celebrated when God put this curse upon the descendant of Solomon—the ruling line and the supposed line that the Messiah would come from. This man was the ancestor of Joseph, the husband of Mary, and is named in the genealogy of Jesus in Matthew. Satan must have thought that he had finally tainted the line of the Messiah and thwarted God's ultimate plan. But, alas, when Jesus sits on the throne of David as the ruling king, he will not be under this curse because he is not of the "seed of Jechoniah." He is no blood relative to Joseph and, therefore, no blood relative to Jechoniah. Satan's plans never come to fruition the way he intends, praise God!

The last genealogy is the one in the book of John. While Matthew presents Christ as king, Mark presents him as servant, and Luke presents him as man, but John presents him as God. All of these are true. So what is the genealogy of God? It is the genealogy of time past from an eternity past. "In the beginning was the Word, and the Word was with God, and the Word was God. The same was in the beginning with God. All things were made by him; and without him was not anything made that was made" (John 1:1–3). "And the Word was made flesh, and dwelt among us and we beheld his glory, the glory as of the only begotten of the father, full of grace and truth" (John 1:14). John does have a genealogy of our Lord, but as you can see, it is the story of his eternal status: Jesus presented as God. He is man, servant, king, and God. He is also the Word, and God would not, therefore, allow mere mortal men to corrupt his Word! It is inspired, inerrant, and complete.

Do you want a relationship with Christ? Do you want to know him more fully? Understand him better? Grow closer to him and he to you? Then study the Word because Christ *is* the Word. You cannot know him and not know the Word. He wants you to know him, that's why he gave us the Word!

In the process of studying both halves of our Bible together, the question may arise, "How do we know the Bible is complete?" A careful look at the messages in both Genesis and Revelation will show finality in this work of art and tie the beginning to the end.

Genesis (the beginning)	Revelation (the ending)
The earth was created in Genesis 1:1: "In the beginning God created the heaven and the Earth."	The earth passes in Revelation 21:1: "And I saw a new heaven and a new earth; for the first heaven and the first earth were passed away; and there was no more sea."
The sun governs the day. Genesis 1:16 says, "And God made two great lights; the greater light to rule the day, and the lesser light to rule the night; he made stars also."	In the end, there will be no more need for the sun. Revelation 21:23 says, "And the city had no need of the sun, neither of the moon, to shine in it: for the glory of God did lighten it, and the Lamb is the light thereof."
Darkness was called night. Genesis 1:5 says, "And God called the light Day, and the darkness he called Night. And the evening and the morning were the first day.	There will be no more night. Revelation 22:5 says, "And there shall be no night there; and they need no candle, neither light of the sun; for the Lord God giveth them light: and they shall reign for ever and ever."
The sea was created in Genesis 1:9: "And God said, Let the waters under the heaven be gathered together unto one place, and let the dry land appear: and it was so."	There will be no more sea in the eternal state. Revelation 21:1 says, "And I saw a new heaven and a new earth; for the first heaven and the first earth were passed away; and there was no more sea."
The beginning of sin and the curse was pronounced in Genesis 3:6: "And when the woman saw that the tree was good for food, and that it was pleasant to the eyes, and a tree to be desired to make one wise, she took of the fruit thereof, and did eat, and gave also unto her husband with her; and he did eat."	Revelation shows the end of sin and the end of the curse. Revelation 22:3 says, "And there shall be no more curse; but the throne of God and of the Lamb shall be in it; and his servants shall serve him."

The entrance of death into the world was also in Genesis. Genesis 3:19 says, "In the sweat of thy face shalt thou eat bread, till thou return unto the ground; for out of it wast thou taken; for dust thou art, and unto dust shalt thou return."	There will be no more death. Revelation 21:4 says, "And God shall wipe away all tears from their eyes; and there shall be no more death, neither sorrow, nor crying, neither shall there be any more pain: for the former things are passed away.
Man was driven out of Eden, Genesis 3:23: "Therefore the LORD God sent him forth from the garden of Eden, to till the ground from whence he was taken."	Man is restored into fellowship and communion with God. Revelation 21:3 says, "And I heard a great voice out of heaven saying, Behold, the tabernacle of God is with men, and he will dwell with them, and they shall be his people, and God himself shall be with them, and be their God."
The tree of life is guarded and not accessible to man. Genesis 3:24 says, "So he drove out the man; and he placed at the east of the garden of Eden Cherubim's, and a flaming sword which turned every way, to keep the way of the tree of life."	We will again have access to the tree of life. Rev 22:2 says, "In the midst of the street of it, and on either side of the river, was there the tree of life, which bare twelve manner of fruits, and yielded her fruit every month: and the leaves of the tree were for the healing of the nations."
Sorrow and suffering entered. Genesis 3:16 says, "Unto the woman he said, I will greatly multiply thy sorrow and thy conception; in sorrow thou shalt bring forth children; and thy desire shall be to thy husband, and he shall rule over thee."	There will be no more sorrow. Revelation 21:4 says, "And God shall wipe away all tears from their eyes; and there shall be no more death, neither sorrow, nor crying, neither shall there be any more pain: for the former things are passed away."
Nimrod founds Babylon and constructs the Tower of Babel in Genesis chapter 11.	Babylon is destroyed in Revelation chapter 12.
God's flood destroyed an evil generation in Noah's time in Genesis chapter 8.	Satan's flood will attempt to destroy the elect generation in Revelation chapter 12.
Genesis is about the first Adam.	Revelation is about the last Adam.

In Genesis, man lost his dominion to Satan.	In Revelation, man regained his dominion from Satan.
Genesis tells us the beginning of the story. The beginning of all things is written in this book.	Revelation tells us the end of the story. The completion of all things is written in this book.

Again, the Old and New Testaments are unified in their message and consistent in the telling. The Bible is not a history of a people, though it does contain an incredible amount of history. It is the story of Christ and his relationship, throughout time, with man. Revelation completes this story of Christ and gives us a brief look at what our eternity with the Lord will be like. There is no need for further Scriptures. God has given us all of the information we require to know him and have a relationship with him. But first, we have to read it, search it, and get to know our Lord through it.

Like an onion has its many layers, so too does the Bible. As we dig into the Scriptures, the divine nature becomes more apparent. Over the course of the 1400–1800 years the Bible was written and the forty separate authors that were involved in this process, there is an interconnectedness that is profound. The absurdity of so many authors working independently and creating such a complex work with absolute consistency without the inspiration of God becomes more apparent the deeper we dig into the hidden meanings in the Scripture. This unity is undeniable and is only identified when the Old and New Testaments are studied together.

Second Timothy 3:16 states, "All scripture is given by the inspiration of God, and is profitable for doctrine, for reproof, for correction, for instruction in righteousness." Our sovereign God, with his complex nature, has a deep and abiding love for us, and because of that love, he has exposed His nature and his very essence for us to see and know through his Word.

Nothing so worthy or so dense with all-encompassing meaning can be perceived without looking just beneath the surface.

CHAPTER 2

Similitudes in Genesis

J ust as God used the names in Genesis 5 to create a model of what was to come, he also used "types" in the Old Testament to give us a foreshadowing of Christ. Hosea 12:10 says, "I have also spoken by the prophets, and I have multiplied visions, and used similitudes by the ministry of the prophets." God is expressing to us the various methods he uses to speak to the people, and one of His methods is "similitudes." God has given us a shockingly accurate picture of our Lord by using stories to point to similarities to the Messiah. The Lord used parables in the New Testament to help his disciples understand his teachings while confusing those not truly interested in the truth. In the Old Testament, he used types or similitudes to give a foreshadowing of what was to come to those desiring his wisdom and willing to look for it while keeping the message disguised against those not truly seeking.

It is important to understand that though we see a lot of symbolism in the Bible and though studying the types involves the understanding of the symbolism, this does not, in any way, imply that the Bible is only symbolic. The first key to interpreting the Bible, while not falling into false doctrine, is to take the Bible first literally, when literal meanings make sense, then symbolically. The stories and situations, people and places of the Bible are real and really happened. That doesn't mean, however, that God did not want us to analyze and understand the symbolism he inserted into Scripture. Also, when coming to conclusions about what the types are symbolizing, it is important to be consistent with all of Scripture. God's Word is without error, without contradiction, balanced and unified.

Nothing replaces good old-fashioned hard work in the process of interpreting the Bible. Second Timothy 2:15 says, "Study to shew thyself approved unto God, a workman that needeth not to be ashamed, rightly dividing the word of truth." Through study, we will divide the truth and thereby deepen our relationship with Christ by getting to know Him better. Second Peter 1:20–21 tells us, "Knowing this first, that no prophecy of the scripture is of any private interpretation. For the prophecy came not in old time by the will of man: but holy men of God spake as they were moved by the Holy Ghost." Interpretation is done through hard work and is available for all. It is not reserved for some private "mystical" interpretation. The interpretation is there in the Bible for all readers to employ. The writing process itself was inspired by the Holy Spirit, and nothing is included or excluded from the written Word without reason and intent. We must stay within the parameters of Scripture and let the Bible interpret the Bible.

We see many examples of types starting very early on in Genesis. Our first example of a foreshadowing is in Genesis 1. The trinity is exposed to us in the very beginning of God's Word. "In the beginning God…" Let's stop there. The Hebrew word for God is *Elohim*, which is plural, Gods. This is a shadowing of the trinity. How do we know that it is only one God when it says Gods? After that, it says, "In the beginning God (Elohim) created…" Stop right there. The word *created* is a singular form of the word in Hebrew. Although the English language does not always have singular and plural forms and agreements between nouns and verbs, the Hebrew language always has noun and verb agreement in regard to a singular or plural form. But not in this verse. It appears to be a grammatical error, but in truth, again, the apparent error shows balance and inspiration. It is plural beings but one God. We go on. We'll try to finish verse 1. "In the beginning God created the heaven and the earth." Verse 2 says, "And the earth was without form and void and darkness was upon the face of the deep. And the Spirit of God moved upon the face of the waters." Okay, we've seen the representation of the trinity hinted at in the contrast between Elohim and the singular version of created; now, we see the Spirit of God moving, and this is the Holy Spirit—one of the Trinity shown separate. Verse 3 says, "And God said, Let there be light; and there was light." "And God said" is the Word of God, and according to John 1:1–3, 14, we know that the Word of God is Christ and that he created everything; now we've seen the Son presented as a separate being, though also part of the Godhead. Verse 4 says, "And God saw the light…" and now we see God the Father. Right off the bat, God has given us a visual of the complete picture of God: three as one then the Spirit, the Son, and the Father.

This concept of the Trinity, though difficult to grasp, is an important concept and a doctrinal foundation. Genesis 1:26 shows the Trinity of God creating the trinity of man. "And God said, Let *us* make man in *our* image, after *our* likeness…" Each part of the Trinity of God created his likeness within the trinity of man and patterned that part of us after that part of Him. We are made of body, soul, and spirit. First Thessalonians 5:23 says, "And the very God of peace sanctify you wholly; and I pray God your whole spirit and soul and body be preserved blameless unto the coming of our Lord Jesus Christ." When we were created in the image of God in Genesis, it wasn't because we were made with two legs and two arms or that Adam was made a man like God. It wasn't our appearance but our completeness. We, like God, are made a trinity. No other creature in God's creation is said to be a trinity; no other creature is it said that they were made after *our* (God's) likeness—only man.

The analysis of our trinity must be based on the analysis of God's Trinity since it was patterned after him. Certainly, our body correlates to Christ who was made flesh for us (John 1:14). Our body has five senses or ways of accumulating information: seeing, smelling, tasting, hearing, and touching. Our body is not perfect, so it's difficult imagining it correlating to the body of Christ, but our resurrection body will be perfect. It is this first one that has all of the problems. At the first coming of Christ, his body also died. This interpretation is also consistent with the verses that tell us that we are the body of Christ. We are his bride and his body just as Eve was the bride of Adam but also flesh of his flesh and bone of his bones. Christ is the body of the Godhead, and we have a body also—someday, a perfect body rather than a temporary shell. Adam and Eve's bodies were created to be eternal, but the fall ruined that original design. Our resurrection bodies, however, will be eternal.

The spirit part of us correlates to the Holy Spirit. To determine what my spirit controls, I analyze the job and duties and attributes of the Holy Spirit because ours was made in the image of his. It has been said that our spirit has five portals just as does our body. They could be defined as worship, prayer, hope in the resurrection, faith in eternity, and reverence. This is a reasonable list that is consistent with Scripture and at least gives us a concept of the job of our spirit. It is eternal and never dies.

The soul aspect of our being thus correlates to the Father of the godhead. Our soul is our definition or personality—what makes me unique. It contains five attributes as well: imagination, memory, conscience, reason, and affection. I don't know that everyone would pick the exact same five attributes, but these five are not inconsistent with Scripture and provide us with a good grasp of the difference between our soul.

No other creation is created as a trinity. The animals have a body and a soul. They have memory, imagination, affection, and reason—a personality. Thus, they have a soul. It's quite clear they have a body. But they have no spirit. Animals do not pray nor do they worship God; they don't hold hope for the resurrection nor do they have faith in eternity. They are not a trinity. Angels have a spirit and a soul; they do not have a body. They clearly have memory, affection, reason, imagination—the attributes of a soul. If they did not, we would not have seen Satan fall nor see him perpetually changing his plan, etc. They certainly have a spirit: they worship God, have faith in eternity, etc. But angels are spirits and thus do not have a body. I realize that they appear to man in a visible form on occasion in the Scriptures, but they are temporary appearances, not permanent bodies. Only man is made in the image of God—a trinity. This is possibly the reason that Satan was jealous and wanted to be like God because he wasn't made a trinity.

In Genesis 3, we see a phenomenal foreshadowing of the relationship between man and God, including the foreshadowing of the salvation story. The story of Adam and Eve is the story of human nature as well as God's nature. Adam and Eve began their trouble by disbelieving the "word" that God gave to them. They allowed themselves to be swayed by Satan's half-truths because that was what they wanted to believe. Remember that Satan, the father of lies, will get more people to believe him if his lies are wrapped in just enough truth to disguise the lie. Their inability to keep the one and only law of God opened their eyes to their sin or "nakedness." Every part of them was laid bare.

Likewise, we begin our troubles with God by disbelieving God's Word as absolute truth. The world around us is constantly attacking the legitimacy of the Bible. Some will use science to try to debunk the validity of the Word of God, though science has actually done more to confirm the inerrancy of the Bible than to debunk it. Archaeology and history have also confirmed the Bible's truths over the years. Yet in spite of the overwhelming number of confirmations, skeptics continue to treat the Bible as a fairy-tale book. Many shows on the mainstream media would rather credit aliens with the intelligence of man and the evolution of nature than give God credit for the creation. The ridiculousness of many of the worldly views is almost comical, yet they continue to imply that all who would believe the Scriptures as fact are fools.

We too are often swayed by Satan's half-truths. Satan begins his lies with pieces of the truth to add credibility to the lies. Often, when we see a piece of truth, especially when it's a piece we want to believe anyway, we are willing and even eager to accept it. In order to lend legitimacy to the half-truth that we wish to continue to believe in, we will then accept the lies that follow without any further investigation. This is the trap that Eve fell into. She wanted to believe Satan's half-truth, so she simply accepted it rather than thinking it through and taking it to God to determine what directions God would have her go. She didn't rely on God's word; she made the decision herself and justified her actions.

Our inability to keep God's law is what opens our eyes to sin and, therefore, our need for a savior. Through our sin, we feel exposed and ashamed, and we have a natural tendency to *not* want to confess our wrongdoing. In Genesis, Adam and Eve hid because of their vulnerability and shame, and we often, in our sin, try to hide from God. When we find ourselves living a lifestyle of sin, we don't want to stay in the steady presence of God. We find ourselves not reading the Word of God, not attending church, and, sometimes, even distancing ourselves from our Christian friends. We want to hide our sin from God, hide our shame and nakedness from the eyes of the Lord just as Adam and Eve tried to do. Of course, God knows where you are, and you can't hide from him. This isn't a threat; it's encouragement because we know that he is there for us in our time of need even when we think we don't want him so close by.

Adam and Eve's next response to their sin is also indicative to our own nature. They attempted to fix the problem themselves rather than taking it to the Lord. It's pretty tough to ask God for help if we are busy trying to hide our sin from him, so we convince ourselves that we can fix the sin ourselves. Whether it's an attempt to create clothing out of fig leaves or an attempt to work out our salvation through works or pay the penalty of sin through our own suffering, all methods that are based in us and not God's are insufficient. Blaming others for our sins, as Adam and Eve did, are also insufficient and actually hinder our ability to get back into a right relationship with God. We see the nature of mankind played out in the actions and motives of Adam and Eve in the very beginning of Genesis.

What about the nature of God? Do these stories reveal to us anything regarding the nature of God? The first thing we should note is that God's original intent was for God and mankind to have an intimate relationship based on love and respect. God walked and talked with Adam in the garden on a daily basis. He provided Adam with all of his needs. The next significant finding we have regarding the nature of God is that he was not satisfied with Adam's attempts to pay for his own sins. The fig leaves were unacceptable to God, and they did not hide Adam's nakedness sufficiently. These qualities are still inherent in God today. He wishes to have a personal relationship with man built on love and respect. And he still does not find our solutions to sin to be acceptable. Just as in the days of Adam, the sin must be paid for with the blood of sacrifice. God, however, provided that blood himself. In Adam's day, God himself provided the skin covering, and therefore, the Lord was the first to offer a sacrifice. He spilled the blood, showing Adam the example of what God expected and how Adam's sins (and those of his descendants) must be paid for. The blood of bulls and goats was never intended to wash away sin but only to cover it until the day of the final sacrifice—that of our Lord and Savior. The sacrifice that was began after the first sin of man, even that sacrifice was only a foreshadowing of what was to come. Just as God himself killed this first animal to clothe Adam and Eve, in His grace, he also presented the sacrifice of Christ himself that his blood may wash away our sins. John 10:18 indicates that Christ *gave* his life; it was not taken from him. "No man taketh it from me, but I lay it down of myself. I have power to lay it down, and I have power to take it again. This commandment have I received of my Father."

Adam and Eve were literal people, and the events in the story truly happened. In addition to this initial understanding, we see types within the framework of the story that foreshadow many aspects of our relationship with Christ. The need for Christ is represented in the story through our inability to keep the law of God's Word just as Adam and Eve did not believe the word of God and did not obey the one command given them. We also see the inadequacies in any attempt we make in our "natural" flesh to pay for our sins and the necessity of the sacrifice. Only through acceptance of this sacrifice can the skins hide our nakedness. Adam and Eve's experiences are a foreshadowing of Christ intended to help us see the right way to begin a relationship with the Lord.

We see a similar theme in the story of Cain and Abel in Genesis chapter 4. Cain brought an offering to God, and being a tiller of the ground, it was fruit of his labor. Abel brought an offering as well, and being a shepherd, he brought a lamb. God honored Abel's offering but not Cain's. Well, before we start bringing God our own offerings, we should learn what type of offering God desires. Cain should have spent a little time getting to know God's expectations before he acted rashly. The first problem with Cain's offering was that it was offered in pride. It was the fruit of *Cain's* labor. In order for Cain to offer a sacrifice other than the one he did, he would have had to humble himself to go to his younger brother to acquire a lamb. Also, Cain chose not to recognize the example set by God himself in Adam and Eve's life, or he was unwilling to follow it. God provided the example of the blood sacrifice by killing the first animal and providing clothes for Cain's parents. But Cain did not choose to follow this pattern. He was not respected for his choice of sacrifice.

Hebrews 11:4 tells us, "By faith Abel offered unto God a more excellent sacrifice than Cain, by which he obtained witness that he was righteous, God testifying of his gifts: and by it he being dead yet speaketh." So we see that Abel's offering was done in faith. His faith led him to offer the blood sacrifice as God required. No doubt Abel did not understand the import of his actions. God had a bigger picture in mind than this one offering, and understanding the sacrifice of animals was supposed to pave the way for the First Coming of Christ. He was sent to die for the sins of the world, to be the ultimate sacrifice, once and for all. Hebrews 9:12–14 says,

> Neither by the blood of goats and calves, but by his own blood he entered in once into the holy place, having obtained eternal redemption for us. For if the blood of bulls and of goats, and the ashes of an heifer sprinkling the unclean, sanctifieth to the purifying of the flesh: How much more shall the blood of Christ, who through the eternal Spirit offered himself without spot to God, purge your conscience from dead works to serve the living God?

It was only the *model* of the true plan of redemption. The blood of Christ washes it away completely. The blood of Christ *is* the true plan of redemption. Without acceptance of the sacrifice, there is no other way to please God.

Just as in the account of Adam and Eve, the account of Cain and Abel also reveals the wicked nature of man. Cain grew quite angry when God accepted his brother's offering and not his own. Even though Cain knew perfectly well that he was acting on his own and not in a manner acceptable to God, he was mad when God did not accept his works in exchange for obedience. First John 3:12 lets us know why Cain killed his brother Abel and gives us a bird's-eye view into Cain's heart. "Not as Cain, who was of that wicked one, and slew his brother. And wherefore slew he him? Because his own works were evil, and his brother's righteous." Jealousy over his brother's obedience to God caused Cain to slay his own brother. I see this same tendency in today's world. Atheists strive to kill the faith of Christians. And what do they offer the world in exchange for a Christian belief in the one true God? Absolutely nothing. No hope for the future, no hope for an afterlife, no solutions to daily problems. They simply want to kill the faith of those around them. They are angry and jealous of the faith and hope they see in the lives of believers.

The account of Noah's ark is full of God's models and the message of salvation, grace, and mercy. Noah and his family were being saved from the judgment to come—a judgment reserved for those rebellious against God and wicked in their heart. The method of their salvation came in the shape of an ark. So Noah is a "type" of a true believer. The ark is a "type" of Christ because it represents salvation from judgment. The ark saves Noah from the coming judgment just as Christ saves us from God's judgment. Though the ark only held eight people and the animals, it was far from full. There was ample room for many more people. And the ark sat for a week before God closed the door, allowing time for others to repent, thus showing God's patience as well as his mercy (Genesis 6:4).

God brought the animals to Noah. Noah didn't have to round them up. God shut the door to keep Noah safe. The door is also symbolic of Christ. John 10:9 says, "I am the door; by me if any man enter in, he shall be saved, and shall go in and out, and find pasture." All those saved from the flood entered into the ark through the door, and when they went out, they found pasture. We are secured and safe in our salvation. When we enter the ark, God closes the door with the Holy Spirit putting God's seal upon our foreheads just as he sealed the door of the ark so long ago. "And grieve not the Holy Spirit of God, whereby ye are sealed unto the day of redemption" (Ephesians 4:30). We'll not be getting out of the ark until God lets us out to find pasture in an eternal state. The ark is built, the door open, the floods held back, but it does us no good if we're not willing to step onto the ark.

In addition to Christ being the ark and the door, he is also the rainbow. Ezekiel 1:26–28 has a beautiful description of Christ on his throne. Verse 28 says, "As the appearance of the bow that is in the cloud in the day of rain, so was the appearance of the brightness round about. This was the appearance of the likeness of the glory of the LORD. And when I saw it, I fell upon my face, and I heard a voice of one that spake." It uses the same word for bow as in Genesis 9:13: "I do set my bow in the cloud, and it shall be for a token of a covenant between me and the earth." Again in Revelation 4:2–3, we see a picture of Christ on his throne: "And he that sat was to look upon like a jasper and a sardine stone: and there was a rainbow round about the throne, in sight like unto an emerald." The rainbow was the unconditional covenant God made with Noah. Christ is the unconditional covenant God made with us, if we'll only get on the ark.

You see, God does it all. He gave Noah the instructions for the ark just as he gave us his Word to direct us to Christ. He brought the animals to Noah, shut the door, dried the waters, regrew the vegetation, told Noah when to leave, and gave him a rainbow. Likewise, the Holy Spirit guides us to salvation and God gives us the faith, offered the sacrifice, and then seals us until the day of redemption. The salvation gift is free to us; God has done it all. Romans 6:23 says, "For the wages of sin is death; but the gift of God is eternal life through Jesus Christ our Lord." All we have to do is accept the gift. *All aboard!*

Another example of God's mercy during this time period is the life of Noah's grandfather: Methuselah, whose name means "his death shall bring." His death brought the flood, and the fact that he lived longer than anyone else in the Bible at 969 years is an indicator of

God's mercy. God wishes none to perish: "The Lord is not slack concerning his promise, as some men count slackness; but is long-suffering to us-ward, not willing that any should perish, but that all should come to repentance," (2 Peter 3:9). But of course, many choose not to receive the free gift of eternal redemption, and God will not take back the gift of free will if we choose unwisely.

These particular similitudes are consistent with all Scripture and provide us with a very personal interpretation of Noah's account that helps us to see the purpose of having it written down for us to read. It's not there just to provide our children with a fun bedtime story, though it certainly is a great story we want to share with our children. The Bible is so much more than that. God is sending us the message of redemption through signs in his Word.

There are other sets of "types" in the account of Noah's ark that pertain to the end of the ages. Matthew 24:37 says, "But as the days of Noah were, so shall also the coming of the Son of man be." This provides scriptural evidence that the story of Noah is a type that correlates to the end-times and the Second Coming of Christ as well as being a literal account of events that occurred. There are multiple ways that this single scripture is played out. The type of people in existence and their relationship with the spirit world is the first one. Though I will mention it here, I will explain it in depth in chapter 3. It is complicated and deep enough to justify its own chapter. According to Genesis chapter 6, the people in Noah's day were cohabitating with angelic beings, evil ones of course, and producing an evil race. This is a very controversial topic, but there is much scriptural evidence to support this theory, and that evidence is presented in the following chapter. Scripture goes on to indicate this same theme will be apparent in the end-times. It is this very practice of angelic beings cohabitating with the daughters of man that results in the seemingly extreme measures God takes to judge the people on a worldwide scale, even the children. This is true in both scenarios: that of Noah's time and the end-times.

The flood of Noah's day is a type of the seven-year tribulation period that we are warned is coming in the end of times. It will directly precede Christ's second coming (Matthew 24). This tribulation period is worldwide (Daniel 7:23) as was the flood of Noah's day (Genesis 8:9). Matthew 24:37–39 again correlates Noah's time period with the Great Tribulation.

> But as the days of Noah were, so shall also the coming of the Son of man be. For as in the days that were before the flood they were eating and drinking, marrying and giving in marriage, until the day that Noah entered into the ark, and knew not until the flood came, and took them all away; so shall also the coming of the Son of man be.

Both global tribulation periods are God's judgment on wicked man. The ark protected Noah and his family during the global flood. He and his family were sealed in the ark. The correlation to this in the end-times is the seal God puts on the forehead of the 144,000 Jews. In Revelation chapter 7, the 144,000 are witnesses to the world during the tribulation period: 12,000 from each of the 12 tribes. According to Revelation 7:3–4, the witnesses are sealed with the seal of God, and it appears to protect them physically as well as spiritually (Revelation 9:4). Only this specific group of Jews is sealed, not all Jews and not all believers. "And I heard the number of them which were sealed: and there were sealed an hundred and forty and four thousand of all the tribes of the children of Israel" (Revelation 7:4).

If all believers are sealed and protected during the tribulation period, then there would be no one martyred for the sake of Christ during this period; they would be protected. This is not the case because the Bible very clearly teaches that many tribulation saints are martyred because of their belief in Christ.

> And when he had opened the fifth seal, I saw under the altar the souls of them that were slain for the word of God and for the testimony which they held: and they cried with a loud voice, saying, How long, O Lord, holy and true,

> dost thou not judge and avenge our blood on them that dwell on the earth? And white robes were given unto every one of them; and it was said unto them, that they should rest yet for a little season, until their fellow servants also and their brethren, that should be killed as they were, should be fulfilled. (Revelation 6:9–11)

This is a picture of saints martyred during the Great Tribulation. More tribulation martyrs are pictured in Revelation 7:9–17. Unlike any other believers during the Tribulation Period, this group of 144,000 witnesses are sealed and protected during the Great Tribulation period come upon the whole world, and likewise, Noah and his family are sealed in the ark, protected from the Great Tribulation period come upon the whole world in Noah's day.

The 144,000 are the only ones specifically mentioned in the Bible to have God's protective seal on their forehead *during the tribulation period*, and yet, we are also sealed. Ephesians 4:30 says, "And grieve not the Holy Spirit of God, whereby ye are sealed unto the day of redemption." We are not only sealed but also we are sealed unto the day of redemption. In spite of surface appearances, the Bible is never inconsistent. There is a difference between us: the 144,000 and the tribulation saints. We must define the various groups of people referred to in the Scriptures, namely, the Gentiles, the Jews, and the church. We don't want to make the mistake of assuming that all of God's chosen people are the same. The difference between the Jews, God's chosen people, and the church, also God's chosen people, is an important concept that must be understood to correctly interpret the Bible. Just because the two groups are both chosen doesn't mean that they are chosen for the same purpose. I may choose one of my children to wash the dishes and another to dry. Both are chosen; one is not better than another or "more chosen." They are simply different.

We'll use the Bible to interpret the Bible and look at biblical examples. From Adam to Abraham, there was no specifically "chosen" lineage. There were only gentiles, some believing, some not. From the time that God made his covenant with Abraham, that his seed through his son Isaac would be a called and chosen generation, there became two groups of people: the Jews (chosen) and the gentiles. Some gentiles were believers, Ruth and Rahab for example, and were incorporated into God's people. His grace has always been apparent even in the Old Testament.

At the day of Pentecost, a new group, a "mystery of Christ" (Eph 3:4), also known as the church, came into the picture. The church is a mystery never mentioned in the Old Testament and not understood by the Jews. Jesus alludes to the mystery in Matthew 13 as he spoke to the disciples in parables. Paul explains this mystery in Ephesians 3:3–6:

> How that by evolution he made known unto me the mystery (as I wrote afore in few words, Whereby, when ye read, ye may understand my knowledge in the mystery of Christ) Which in other ages was not made known unto the sons of men, as it is now revealed unto his holy apostles and prophets by the Spirit; That the Gentiles should be fellow heirs, and of the same body, and partakers of his promise in Christ by the gospel.

The concept that multitudes of gentiles could be chosen by God not because of their lineage and relation to Abraham but simply because they believed was a bizarre and radical view to the Jews. The church itself was born on the day of Pentecost—the day the Holy Spirit no longer operated in his Old Testament role of temporarily "filling" a believer for a specific duty but rather became the indweller who lives within the believer at all times.

The church that began on the day of Pentecost was not a specific building or denomination. It is made up of believers in the resurrection of Jesus Christ. This is also a chosen group—chosen for a different purpose than the Jews. While the Jews were the wife of Yahweh in the Old Testaments and were called to bring forth the Messiah, the church is called to be the spotless bride of Christ. The Jews were chosen to be the repository for the oracles of God by bringing us the

Old Testament with its emphasis on the justice of God. Meanwhile, the church is called to be the repository for the oracles of God by bringing forth the New Testament, with its emphasis on the grace of God. The Jews were called because God wanted to keep the promise of Abraham (Deuteronomy 7:6) while the church was chosen for God to call out a people for his name (Acts 15:19). The word *church* is not mentioned in the Bible until Matthew 16:18, and even then, the reference is future. Christ said, "Upon this rock I *will* build my church." At the time of this conversation between Peter and Christ, it hadn't been built yet. The word *church* is not mentioned in any of the other gospels. From Acts onward, the word *church* becomes commonplace in Scripture because the church is born at Pentecost. The Jews and the church are two separate groups called for two separate purposes. The tribulation saints are in the same category as the Jews, but they are saved during the tribulation period.

Back to Noah's family, they are a type of the 144,000 in the end-times. What about the church? Why aren't they sealed for protection during the tribulation period? Well, during Noah's time, there was a godly man named Enoch. He was not a Jew because there were no Jews or chosen generations before Abraham. Enoch was a believing gentile. Enoch was born the same day as the church on the same day that would be Pentecost thousands of years before there was a Pentecost. Enoch is a *type* of the church.

In addition to Enoch's *coincidental* birthday being on the same day as the birthday of the church, Enoch's name means "teaching." This is what we, the members of the church, are supposed to be doing: teaching people about the Lord. Before the flood came, Genesis 5:24 says, "And Enoch walked with God: and he was not; for God took him." Hebrews 11:5 tells us, "By faith Enoch was translated that he should not see death; and was not found, because God had translated him: for before his translation he had this testimony, that he pleased God." Enoch was raptured before the flood. As a type of the church, Enoch's disappearance is just one of the indicators that the church will be raptured before the tribulation period. Enoch was also raptured on the day of Pentecost. Could this be coincidence? I don't believe there are any coincidences in God's Word. Since the church will not be present on earth during the tribulation period, the tribulation saints cannot be members of the church. All of those saved during this worldwide judgment period, and there will be many, are known as tribulation saints, and many are martyred for the sake of Christ.

The symbolism, by no means, minimizes the truth of the actual events of the Bible. The events occurred exactly as the Bible states, and the people within the Bible have free will to choose the direction of their lives. At the same time, God orchestrated the events in the Bible according to his foreknowledge of events and people's reactions and according to his sovereignty. He intentionally left out pieces of the history and the lives of the people that were not relevant to his story. The parts God did record in his word are relevant to us and to Christ, and we should strive to read, learn, and understand them. The types or similitudes that Hosea referred to in chapter 12 verse 10 and that we see repeated in Scripture have a two-fold nature. God uses them to reveal his plan to those willing to look for it and in a similar manner to that in which Christ used the parables of the New Testament. These types also testify of the accuracy of the inspired Word of God.

CHAPTER 3

Nephilim

The account of Noah's ark and the destruction of mankind through the flood gives us enormous insight into the destruction of the last days. Using New Testament references to the flood and tying them together with Genesis helps us answer some tough questions regarding the nature of God also. Why did God send the flood? Why did he wipe out all mankind except Noah and his family? Was Noah really more righteous than the infants that had not yet had an opportunity to sin? How does this story relate to today's world? When it says, "As in the days of Noah were, so shall the coming of the Son of man be" (Matthew 24:37). What exactly does that mean? What should we be looking for?

Genesis chapter 6 is an interesting description of conditions before the flood. In verse 2, it says, "That the sons of God saw the daughters of men that they were fair; and they took them wives of all which they chose." Verses 4–5 goes on to say,

> There were giants [*Nephilim*] in the earth in those days; and also after that, when the sons of God came in unto the daughters of men, and they bare children to them, the same became mighty men of renown. And God saw that the wickedness of man was great in the earth, and that every

imagination of the thoughts of his heart was only
evil continually. (Italics mine)

The word *giants* is a mistranslation. The Hebrew word is
Nephilim which means "fallen ones." Fallen from where? These were
not "big" people or giants, necessarily; they were wicked. When it
says "mighty men of renown," this is not a compliment; it's a description of their wickedness and their wicked deeds.

The first point we are going to tackle is the question, Who
are the sons of God? Some will say that this is an example of being
unequally yoked—the sons of God being descendants of Seth which
are righteous men. This position then says that the daughters of men
were the daughters of Cain and wicked women. Is this consistent
with biblical teaching elsewhere? Does the Bible show clear examples
of righteous men producing a lineage of righteous men? No, unfortu-
nately, we see that many righteous men often produced wicked children, and certainly, their descendants would gradually descend into
unrighteousness. Do biblical examples show that unions between
believers and unbelievers produce men so evil that every imagination of their heart is wicked? Are these wicked people the children of
unequally yoked couples? Would that union produce men of unusual
power (mighty men of renown)? No.

Sometimes, godly men have unbelieving children; sometimes,
evil men have godly children. That is the nature of free will. Why
would we assume that all of Seth's descendants were pure and Cain's
descendants were all wicked? Furthermore, what about Adam and
Eve's other children? Only Cain, Abel, and Seth were named because
their stories are pertinent to God's Word. These three children of
Adam and Eve tell us something in their stories about the nature of
man and God, but Adam and Eve had other children. Where do they
all fit in this picture? The Sethian theory creates more questions than
it answers. There is no scriptural evidence that the sons of God are
descendants of Seth, thus this theory can carry no more weight than
a guess. Let's consult the Scriptures and see what it takes to be labeled
a "son of God."

When we scour the Bible for references to the sons of God, there are four categories, all with one very important thing in common. All Scriptural references where the term "son of God" is used shows a direct creation of God. A son of God is someone who is not a procreation or the result of a reproduction but rather a creation made directly by God.

The first example is Adam. He was not procreated, and in Luke 3:38, in the genealogy of Christ, it says, "Which was the son of Enos, which was the son of Seth, which was the son of Adam, which was the *son of God*." Obviously, the sons of God in Genesis 6 do not fall under the category of this example, so we'll look at the next.

Another person who is said to be the son of God is Jesus Christ. He came from the womb of a woman but was not a procreation of a man and woman but rather the direct creation of God through the Holy Spirit. First John 5:5 says, "Who is he that overcometh the world, but he that believeth that Jesus is the *Son of God*?" And verse 13 of the same chapter goes on to say, "These things have I written unto you that believe on the name of the *Son of God*; that ye may know that ye have eternal life, and that ye may believe on the name of the *Son of God*." Obviously, this is not the sons of God referenced in Genesis 6.

Born-again believers in their regenerated condition are called the sons of God. In our physical body, we are procreations. In our spirit, once we are saved, we are direct creations of God, for we are made new creations in Christ Jesus. We go back to 1 John and read chapter 3 verses 1–2, and we see that it calls us sons of God. "Behold, what manner of love the Father hath bestowed upon us, that we should be called the *sons of God*; therefore the world knoweth us not, because it knew him not." The gospel of John 1:12 says, "But as many as received him, to them gave the power to become the *sons of God*, even to them that believe on his name." Nowhere are any Old Testament saints called the sons of God, only born-again believers in Jesus Christ.

Now, we would certainly all agree that the Old Testament believers were "saved" in a sense, but they were not born-again believers in the death and resurrection of Jesus Christ because Jesus had not yet been born and resurrected. Born-again believers are the bride of Christ or members of the "church" (Revelation 19:7; Mark 2:18–20, 2 Corinthians 11:2). Old Testament saints are the wife of Yahweh (Isaiah 54:5–6). These are two separate groups both chosen by God but for different purposes. But since the sons of God in Genesis 6 are in the Old Testament, they cannot be members of the church. Therefore, this is not the correct category referred to in Genesis.

This leaves the last group of beings ever called the sons of God in the Bible: angels. They are the direct creations of God. In Job 1:6, there is reference to the angels as sons of God. "Now there was a day when the *sons of God* came to present themselves before the Lord, and Satan came also among them." Job 2:1 says, "Again there was a day when the *sons of God* came to present themselves before the Lord and Satan came also among them to present himself before the Lord." And again in Job 38:7, I believe that is what is referred to in Genesis 6. A common argument against this view, that the sons of God who came down and cohabitated with the daughters of men were angels, is that the Bible tells us that angels do not marry. In Mark 12:25 it says, "For when they shall rise from the dead, they neither marry nor are given in marriage but are as the angels which are in heaven." There is a very good reason for angels in heaven not marrying; they are immortal and do not die, and therefore there is no need to reproduce. This is why, I'm sure, God only made male angels. There is no need for females. This does not mean, however, that they cannot choose to rebel against God's design and procreate with a woman.

Is there any scriptural evidence indicating that it is possible for angels to engage in such human activities like cohabitation? Well, actually, yes. There are several good scriptural arguments for this position in both Old and New Testaments. The first is also in Genesis.

In Genesis chapter 19, we find the story of Sodom and Gomorrah. This is another tragic story, like Noah, in which God destroys everyone with no apparent mercy. Well, two angels have entered the city. Lot recognized them immediately for what they were and pressed upon them to stay in his house, even fed them unleavened bread (leaven representing sin), and calls them "my lords," indicating that he understood them to have come from God. Now, the story goes that the men of Sodom demanded that Lot would give these men up so that they might "know them," and we all know that's not a dinner invitation. Apparently, these men all believed that sex with an angel was possible. Furthermore, the angels engaged in other activities of the flesh; they ate and drank with Lot. But, of course, just because the Sodomites believed they could cohabitate with the angels doesn't mean the angels actually could do such a thing. But then, if there were no danger of this sin, why would God (through the hand of the angels) blind these men so that they could not find the door? It wasn't to protect Lot since Lot himself had just been outside and apparently wasn't bothered. It doesn't appear that it was to protect Lot's family since Lot himself offered his daughters to the men, and they weren't interested. I would argue that it was to protect the angels from molestation. These were righteous angels; the ones in Genesis 6 were not. They had "fallen" from their place in the presence of God, had looked upon the beautiful women, and had chosen pleasures of the flesh over glory to God.

If this is all true, what happened to those angels? The angels themselves would not have died in the flood or in the destruction of those wicked cities since angels don't die. Jude 1:6–7 says,

> And the angels *which kept not their first estate*, but left their own habitation, he hath reserved in everlasting chains under darkness unto the judgment of the great day. Even as Sodom and Gomorrah, and the cities about them in like manner, giving themselves over to fornication, and going after *strange flesh*, are set forth for an example, suffering the vengeance of eternal fire.

Wow. So there were a group of angels that kept not their first estate and left their own habitation. They left heaven. Are these angels the third of the angels Satan took with him when he left heaven on that day before creation? Or are they a new group that left later? Well, the reference certainly isn't pertaining to the day Satan left heaven for a couple reasons. First off, most or all of Satan's angels, now called demons, are not chained in darkness until the great judgment day; they are roaming to and fro on the earth doing the work of Satan. And isn't it interesting that it talks about the angels and Sodom and Gomorrah in the same section of Scripture? These angels are chained as an example, just as Sodom and Gomorrah was an example, and both of them are examples of what God will do when you go after strange flesh. The phrasing makes a lot more sense if you understand that strange flesh is not referring to homosexuality but interbreeding between angelic/demonic beings and mankind. That's what was happening that caused the complete destruction of those cities.

Now, I'm not saying they weren't rampant with homosexuality and other sin; they obviously were. But the evil created by this unholy union justified absolute destruction. You see, mankind can repent, and that is certainly God's first choice. Nineveh is an example of God giving a very wicked society the opportunity to repent by sending Jonah. Why didn't God send anyone to the cities of Sodom and Gomorrah? Because angels cannot repent; they have no kinsman redeemer. Christ came as a man to deliver man (Hebrews 2:16–17); he is not part angel. Furthermore, the angels have seen the glory of God firsthand and still chose to rebel. They cannot be redeemed. Therefore, their children cannot repent. They are born with every imagination wicked and have no desire to repent thus requiring complete destruction in both Noah's time and in Sodom and Gomorrah. Remember, God would've spared the city if he only could've found a few righteous people. But he found *none.* I would argue that this even included the children.

In regard to the evil children created by this union, I'd like to look at the phrasing of Gen 6:9: "Noah was a just man and perfect in his *generations.*" Noah's generations or genealogy or lineage was perfect. His family was the only family left on earth that had not been tainted by this ungodly union. That must've been an uncomfortable environment for a godly man to live in and to raise his children in.

Could Noah tell which people were only part human and which were all human? No, I don't believe so. I do not believe the evil children look any different than normal humans. There are a couple of reasons why I hold this view. The reason some people assume that these ungodly creations look different than regular men is because of the references to "giants." But we must remember that giants was an incorrect translation. It is "fallen ones," and it's referring to fallen angels. Hebrews 13:2 says that some have entertained angels unawares, so even the fallen ones may not have been obvious. Also, Noah would not have bothered to preach to the people if he knew that they were all part angel and without the hope of redemption. Do we need to worry that we might accidentally marry someone of this sort without knowledge or the ability to discern? Noah followed God as did his "generations" before him. He may not have been able to look at someone and say, "He's part angel," but there is not much of a temptation to marry someone whose every imagination is wicked unless we are rebellious against God and wicked in our own heart.

Now, turn to 2 Peter 2:4–6:

> For if God spared not the angels that sinned, but cast them down to hell, and delivered them into chains of darkness, to be reserved unto judgment; And spared not the old world but saved Noah the eighth person, a preacher of righteousness, bringing in the flood upon the world of the ungodly; And turning the cities of Sodom and Gomorrah into ashes condemned them with an overthrow, making them an example unto those that after should live ungodly.

It's not a coincidence that the angels that sinned, Noah, and Sodom and Gomorrah are all mentioned in the same passage. Again, these angels that sinned cannot be the third of the angels that Satan took out of heaven with him because these angels are chained until judgment, and Satan's cohorts are not. These angels brought the flood upon the world of the ungodly (verse 5). Their behavior also turned the cities of Sodom and Gomorrah into ashes (verse 6). They are the angels of Genesis 6 that looked upon the daughters of men and bore children with them.

In addition, there is a translational issue that is very relevant to this scripture. The Greeks have more than one word for "hell" while in English, it is always translated into the same word. We only have one word for hell, but in reality, the Greek language made a distinction between the "different" hells as did the Hebrew language. In this particular passage (verse 4), the Greek word was *Tartarus*. It is the only place in the Bible that this word is used; it is the only place in the Bible that this particular location is named. It is a special place in the spirit world that is apparently reserved only for angels like the ones at Noah's time or those in Sodom and Gomorrah. It is a temporary abode since all of death and hell are thrown into the lake of fire (the permanent hell in Revelation 20:14.) These angels that commit the sin of Genesis 6 are thrown into *Tartarus* as a deterrent to other angels, and the flood and destruction of these two specific incidents are an example for mankind of what they have to look forward to should they live ungodly lives (verse 6).

The following are the other references to the other "hells" in the Bible. Sheoul in Hebrew and Hades in Greek is the temporary abode of the wicked dead. It was the place that the rich man was residing in when he spoke to Lazarus and requested a drink (Luke 16:19–31). There was a gulf between Hades and paradise (verse 26); the latter being the place in which Lazarus was residing, and therefore, it was the temporary abode of the righteous dead. This is the place Christ referred to when he told the thief on the cross, "Today you shall be with me in Paradise" (Luke 23:43). Though Hades will not be emptied until death and hell are cast into the lake of fire (Gahenna in Greek, Tophet in Hebrew) at the Great White Throne of Judgment (Revelation 20:14), paradise no longer exists. This temporary abode of the righteous dead was a "holding tank" for the Old Testament saints until the resurrection of Jesus Christ. They could not be in heaven with the Father until their sins were paid for with the death and resurrection of our Lord. They were saved on a credit card, and once it was paid up, Christ descended and emptied paradise and took those souls to heaven (Ephesians 4:8—9). Now, to be absent from the body is to be present with the Lord (2 Corinthians 5:8).

To summarize these various spiritual locations, we recognize the temporary abode of the righteous, paradise, which no longer exists, and the permanent abode of the righteous dead is heaven. We then have two temporary abodes of the wicked dead: Tartarus for angels, Hades or Sheoul for mankind. We also have the eternal hell, Gehenna or lake of fire, which will have no inhabitants until the end of the tribulation period when the Antichrist and the false prophet are the first to be cast in (Revelation 19:20). There is one other spiritual location regarding wickedness, and that is pertinent to Scripture, and that is the *Abusso* in Greek or the Abyss. This is the abode of Satan and the demons where they have the ability to go in and out until Satan is chained in the abyss after the tribulation period (Revelation 9:2, 20:3). Of all these various references to hell in the Bible, the only place Tartarus is mentioned is in 2 Peter 2 and as a prison for this particular group of angels mentioned in 2 Peter 2. This group of angels rebelled against God in an especially wicked way and caused judgment that justified the complete annihilation of the flood and, later, Sodom and Gomorrah.

The next scripture is a complicated scripture that must be analyzed carefully:

> For Christ also hath once suffered for sins, the just for the unjust, that he might bring us to God, being put to death in the flesh, but quickened by the Spirit: By which also he went and preached unto the spirits in prison; Which sometime were disobedient, when once the long-suffering of God waited in the days of Noah, while the ark was a preparing, wherein few, that is, eight souls were saved by water. (1 Peter 3:18–20)

If you will notice in verse 18 that Christ was quickened by the Spirit; that would be the Holy Spirit. The Holy Spirit went to preach to the spirits who are now in prison. Who are the spirits in prison? Let's read the next piece and try to put the puzzle together. "Which sometime were disobedient." Okay, when the word *spirit* is used in other places in the Bible with no modifier, no explanation like "spirit of man" or "spirit of God," etc., it is referring to angels. These spirits were disobedient sometime, and if we read on, we find out when they were disobedient. "When once the long-suffering of God waited in the days of Noah, while the ark was a preparing." So while Noah was building the ark, the spirits were being disobedient and the Holy Spirit (through Noah) was preaching to them.

Remember, God uses a man of God to take the Word of God and create a child of God. God was using Noah. Christ also preached to the Ephesians through someone else: through Paul. In Ephesians 2:17, Paul refers to the time Christ preached peace to them even though Christ was never in Ephesus. He had used Paul as his vessel to deliver his Word, and in Noah's time, God used Noah to deliver his word to the spirits who are now in prison. The spirits are in prison at the time that Peter writes this text, but they were not in prison when they were being preached to. God is not preaching to them while they are in prison; there would be no point. For one thing, the angels/hybrids are not redeemable nor do they want to be. For another, nowhere in the Bible is there any indication that there is salvation after death. Also, they are in "prison." This word makes sense when you look at the other scriptures about the angels who are *chained* in Tartarus, which would be a picture of a prison (2 Peter 2).

The wicked dead of mankind are not chained in Hades. And, of course, we know that Noah was preaching to the wicked while he built the ark. He was preaching to wicked angels as well as their off-spring and wicked humans. After all, the people were not necessarily visibly different from the angel/man hybrids, and though the hybrids and angels would not repent, the women who cohabitated with them could have. Noah would not know who was who in the zoo, and the Holy Spirit worked through Noah to preach to all of the living souls in Noah's time to give anyone a chance at repentance. God, however, did know who was who, and the "long-suffering of God waited in the days of Noah." I believe this is an indication that God was waiting until conditions had so deteriorated that Noah was the only one left who was perfect in his generations.

As long as there was a chance of someone coming to the Lord, God was willing to wait. Just as in Sodom and Gomorrah's time, God promised Abraham that if he could find just a righteous few, he would not destroy the city. But there was no one, not even the hope of children; they were all tainted. And in the days of Noah, only eight souls were saved by water.

The concept that rebellious angels were coming down from the heavens to cohabitate with women might make us a little uncomfortable. In addition to being well-supported by Old and New Testament scriptures, this theory also answers a lot of questions. It explains why a loving and merciful and just God would destroy so many people, many children, in such a thorough manner. It explains the many incidents during Old Testament times that God commanded his army to destroy an entire tribe, women, children, etc. It explains why every living being was seen as expendable in God's eyes in the cities of Sodom and Gomorrah. These people were born wicked without the ability or the desire to repent.

We may scratch our heads trying to figure out why angels would leave the throne of God to indulge in pleasures of the flesh, but didn't Satan consider his desires to be above God's will? Don't we, to a much lesser degree and with less understanding, sometimes leave the peace of being in line with God's will to chase after some fleshly lust or another? Perhaps not a sexual sin, but maybe our fleshly indulgence is gluttony, alcohol, drugs, pride, gossip, or unforgiveness. We, of course, have not stood in the absolute fullness of his glory, but the angels were making a similar choice; they too have free will. They are held more accountable because their knowledge is complete, and that's why God did not send them a kinsman redeemer to save them. If his glory was not sufficient to satisfy these angels, then nothing would bring them to repentance.

This view may answer some questions, but it certainly produces more. If this sin was occurring in Noah's time and certainly repeated in Lot's time at Sodom and Gomorrah, what stops more angels, or some of Satan's angels, from making this same choice? Could it be happening now? I would say that having the previous angels locked in Tartarus as an example might deter some from repeating the mistake. But other than that, there is nothing to stop a repeat of this sin. And yes, I do believe it will happen in the end-times, and I do believe it is happening now. Matthew 24:38–39 says,

> For as in the days that were before the flood they were eating and drinking, marrying and giving in marriage, until the day that Noah entered into the ark, and knew not until the flood came and took them all away; so shall also the coming of the Son of man be.

The Lord was explaining to his disciples the timing of the Second Coming of Christ. He was not discussing the rapture of the church, and all of Matthew 24 and 25 are a description of the tribulation period which precedes the Second Coming. Just as in the days of Noah, they were marrying and giving in marriage before the flood, we will see a resurrection of the same sins before the tribulation period. I believe this is a description of the angels marrying the women, though I recognize that this scripture standing by itself does not specify what types of marriages. My view comes from the other scriptures we've already discussed. Because the scriptures seem to indicate that this was the cause of the flood, then the same circumstances will precede the tribulation period, which is God's judgment upon the whole world (just as in the days of Noah).

I find it interesting the number of movies and television shows that are about this very thing. Many movies made in recent years portray angelic beings who leave their heavenly home and fall in love with an earthly woman. They then give up their immortality to become human. Of course, the angel in question is always the hero of the movie. I don't think such an angel is a hero in God's eyes. This is a more common theme in our society than many of us are aware of, even if you choose to believe that it does not actually occur. Other movies that are common in our era are movies portraying vampires and werewolves falling in love with and intermarrying into the human race. It also brings to mind the characters so common in Greek mythology. They commonly portrayed beings that are half human, half something else. Many of their characters were said to be "sons of the gods." Is it possible that these myths were spawned by the creation of offspring that are actually the sons of demonic beings?

Daniel has an interesting reference to this time period that I believe to be pertinent to our discussion. In Daniel chapter 2, Daniel is given the interpretation of the statue in Nebuchadnezzar's dream. The statue represents various kingdoms throughout history, and Daniel is explaining that Nebuchadnezzar is the head of gold; the Medo-Persian empire is the chest/arms of silver, the belly of brass is the Greek empire, the two legs of iron is the Roman empire (with a western and eastern leg), and then the end-times government will be the feet and toes of iron mixed with miry clay, and last, but certainly not least, is the stone (Christ) that destroys all other kingdoms and becomes the eternal kingdom. In verse 43 (remember the feet and toes of iron mixed with miry clay is the end-times kingdom), it says, "And whereas thou sawest iron mixed with miry clay, they shall mingle themselves with the seed of men: but they shall not cleave one to another, even as iron is not mixed with clay." Well, whoever "they" are, they are apparently not the "seed of men," yet they mingle themselves with the seed of men. I believe this is yet another support for the Nephilim theory and the activities that bring on God's judgment of the whole world.

Understanding the person of the Antichrist is also impacted by the Nephilim theory. Who is this Antichrist? Where does he come from? Is he special or just a regular man? How is he like Judas?

An important issue to understand when trying to figure out where the Antichrist comes from is an understanding of how Satan works and what motivates him. Simply put, Satan wants to be like God; he always has (Isaiah 14:13). That was the original sin even before the creation of man. Anytime we desire to be like someone else, we pursue our goal by mimicking and counterfeiting everything that "someone else" does. Satan is a very motivated counterfeiter. Everything he does is an imitation of God. A common Satanic symbol is a five-pointed star; the Jews have the Star of David with six points. Satanic cults use the same color schemes as the priests of the Old Testament, and they have priests and high priest. God's city is

Jerusalem; Satan's is Babylon. God's Trinity has Father, Son, and Holy Spirit; Satan's trinity has Satan, Antichrist, and false prophet.

We could go on and on with examples of Satan imitating the Almighty, but the one we're interested in discussing is the imitation of the Son. The Holy Spirit came upon Mary, and she was with child. God created his son, and I believe Satan did too. I believe Judas was the literal son of Satan just as Christ is the literal Son of God. Of course, Satan cannot create as God does, but he can procreate. In John 17:12, Judas is called the son of perdition. There are only two people in the entire Bible called the "son of perdition:" Judas and the Antichrist. I'll explain the connection in a moment. But for now, I believe the Bible is literal, and I believe Judas was the son of Satan. I think that when the Holy Spirit came upon Mary, Satan imitated God with the plan to destroy Christ and procreated with a woman thus making a son of perdition.

Satan is not omniscient (all-knowing) and had many backup plans. He tried to destroy the Jews throughout history to prevent the birth of the Messiah. When that didn't work, he tried to use Herod to kill the Messiah as a child. He had a son in imitation of God and used him to try to destroy the Messiah, not understanding the resurrection any better than the disciples did. He is, after all, only an angel.

In Luke 22:3, we find an interesting scripture. The chief priests and scribes are considering how to do away with the Lord, and Satan enters Judas. There is also an account in John 13:27 of Satan incarnating Judas. Now, there are many biblical examples of demons possessing people, but only two people are ever said to be possessed by Satan himself: that's right, Judas Iscariot and the Antichrist. Satan is busy approaching the throne of God to accuse the brethren (Job 1:6) and cannot be in all places at the same time. But he does set the time aside to enter Judas in his attempt to get rid of the Messiah. He uses his own son to try to destroy God's son. Of course, we know the outcome, and with hindsight, we understand the necessity of Christ's death and the victory of his resurrection.

Now, if Judas is an angel/human hybrid, is he then without redemption? Well, it would appear so. In Matthew 27:3–5, it says that Judas "saw he was condemned." This sounds very final, not like it's just Judas's opinion, but it sounds like Judas was condemned indeed. Now, were he a mere man, he would not be without hope, he could still repent. But it doesn't appear that Judas has that option. It goes on to say,

> When he saw that he was condemned, repented himself, and brought again the thirty pieces of silver to the chief priests and elders, saying, I have sinned in that I have betrayed the innocent blood… And he cast down the pieces of silver in the temple, and departed and went and hanged himself.

He apparently did repent to some degree. He knew he was wrong but it did not make a difference in his eternal state. Christ admits having lost Judas in his prayer in Luke chapter 17 verse 12 and in Matthew 26:24. He states, when referring to the man who betrays Christ, "It had been good for that man if he had not been born." This would not be so if Judas's repentance created eternal forgiveness. In Acts 1:24, the disciples wanted to know who would be taking Judas's place "that he may take part of this ministry and apostleship, from which Judas by transgression fell, that he might go to his own place." What an interesting choice of words. Since we've established that Judas went to hell, why would this be called *his own place* unless, as the literal son of perdition, this is where he came from.

In making the connection between Judas and the Antichrist, look at what Genesis 3:15 says, "And I will put enmity between thee and the woman, and between thy seed and her seed." Now, keep in mind that in this section of scripture, God is talking to Satan after Satan has tricked Eve into eating the forbidden fruit. So God is saying he will put enmity between Satan and the woman (Israel) and between Satan's seed and Israel's seed. Well, Israel's seed is the Messiah. Satan has a seed? Well, this makes sense if you believe the Nephilim theory we are presenting. Second Thessalonians 2:3 calls the Antichrist the "son of perdition." Again, I prefer to take the Bible literally unless it's obvious from the text that it was intended to be symbolic; as soon as we start to symbolize, then it becomes subject to all sorts of different interpretations. I don't believe God intends us all to have different interpretations that create different messages, many very inconsistent with each other. The Bible is shockingly consistent, and so is God. If we use the Bible to interpret the Bible instead of every man making up his own interpretation, then we will not get far off the path. So the Antichrist is the literal son of perdition, but so was Judas.

If Satan is trying to imitate God, why does he have two sons? I believe Satan imitated God in creation of Judas in the same historical time period as Christ. He even named his son Judas—the New Testament version of Judah, and of course, Christ is the Lion of the tribe of Judah. Through the Antichrist, he then has a "second coming" of his son in the same historical time period as the Second Coming of our Lord. Again, Satan will attempt to use his son (his second son, this time) to stop God's Son. If he can crush the Jews, then they cannot call out for their Messiah. If they do not call out for their Messiah, Christ will not return (Hosea 5:15). This is Satan's plan, and I do not believe the Antichrist is a normal man. He is evil to the core, without hope of redemption; he is the son of perdition, and just like the offspring in the days of Noah, he will be a mighty man of renown. He is incarnated by Satan himself, just as Judas was, in the middle of the tribulation period. This man is a Nephilim as was his brother before him and as were many throughout our history.

And while watching the evil that goes on today, the children are driven to murder, the increased number of evil deeds that simply makes no sense to anyone including secular psychiatrists, perhaps, we'd be surprised by the Nephilim we are unknowingly surrounded by. But just as Noah preached to them all because he could not discern who was who, we also must continue to preach the Word of God and not give up hope on anyone. Many people who appear beyond redemption have been saved, and we must not begin to assume we can tell the difference. Noah was our example; follow in his footsteps, and don't resign your post.

CHAPTER 4

Patriarchs

Often, a cursory surface look at the stories in the Bible misses pertinent and important facts that will bring us in to a closer relationship with our Lord. Matthew 22:37 tells us, "Jesus said unto him, Thou shalt love the Lord thy God with all thy heart, and with all thy soul, and with all thy mind." The act of loving the Lord with all of our mind involves diligent study, and this will help to bring us closer to God and improve our relationship to him partly through our better understanding of who he is. In our pursuit of understanding Christ, let's look beneath the surface in the lives of Abraham and Isaac, Jacob, and some of his sons. Finally, we'll look at some symbolism in the story of Moses. We'll begin with Abraham, particularly his trial, when God asked him to sacrifice his son, Isaac. We see God continuing to show future generations the details of the coming of Christ in this narrative.

To give a quick background on our story of Abraham, God had called Abraham out of his home in the land of Ur, which is located in modern day Iraq. He called him to take everything he owned and make a new home in the promised land or Israel. God promised to give Abraham a son that would be the father of nations even though Abraham's wife was barren. In Genesis chapter 21, God finally provided Abraham with the son he had promised many years before. Abraham was a hundred years old when Isaac was miraculously born, and Sarah was ninety. It is estimated that Isaac was a teenager when

God came to Abraham in chapter 22 and told Abraham to make the ultimate sacrifice—that of his only son.

Abraham was sent to Mount Moriah for this event. The meaning of Moriah is "my teacher is Yah," Yah being short for Yahweh—one of the names of God Almighty. Indeed, God has much to teach us in the account of Abraham's visit to the mount. When they arrived at Mount Moriah, Abraham asked his servants to wait for him while he and Isaac continued up the mountain alone. Abraham's words to his servants were profound. He said, "Abide ye here with the ass; and I and the lad will go yonder and worship, and come again to you" (Genesis 22:5). Abraham truly was a man of faith, and his faith was in the resurrection. He was going up the mount to sacrifice his son, yet he told his servant that he and the boy would be right back. Abraham knew Isaac was the child of the promise—the child that would bring nations as plentiful as the dust of the earth (Genesis 13:16), and yet God told him to sacrifice this very same son. Abraham believed God would raise Isaac from the dead.

Abraham's faith in the resurrection of the son was profound and a fascinating foreshadowing of an event two thousand years yet to come. In so many ways, Isaac is a type of Christ. The events in his life are a model of events that would one day occur in the life of our Lord. Isaac carried the wood for his own sacrifice up the mountain, and two thousand years later, Christ would walk up this same exact mountain carrying his own cross. Yes, Mount Moriah is Golgotha—the same hill Christ was crucified on.

When God told Abraham to sacrifice Isaac, Abraham was in Beersheba, about forty-eight miles southwest of Jerusalem. They journeyed three days with an entourage, and they could've easily made the forty-eight mile journey to Golgotha in that time period. Some have argued that Mount Moriah is Mount Sinai, but there is no possible way Abraham could've traveled the two hundred miles to Mount Sinai in only three days on foot with just an ass. That would require them to travel about sixty-seven miles a day, which they simply could not have done. Furthermore, in Genesis 22:14, it says, "And Abraham called the name of that place Jehovah-Jireh: as it is said to this day, in the mount of the LORD it shall be seen."

What shall be seen? Notice it is future tense, and at this point in the scripture, Isaac had already been saved by the ram's presence. In the mount of the Lord, the *crucifixion of Christ* shall be seen. In addition, Jehovah-Jireh means "God will provide" once again giving us hints to Christ's provision for the forgiveness of sins. God provides for all mankind through the sacrifice and resurrection of his only son.

Continuing on with our story, Abraham and Isaac reach the top of Mount Moriah, and Isaac asks his father, "Where is the lamb for a burnt offering?" (Genesis 22:7). Abraham responds, "My son, God will provide *himself* a burnt offering" (Genesis 22:8). Is this an indication that Abraham expected God to provide an alternate sacrifice and therefore prevent Isaac's death? Or is it something more prophetic? I don't believe Abraham was referring to a scapegoat for Isaac at all. Abraham had every intention of sacrificing Isaac, and he truly believed God would raise him from the dead. We see this in Genesis 22:12 when God said to Abraham, "And he said, Lay not thine hand upon the lad, neither do thou anything unto him: for now I know that thou fearest God, seeing thou hast not withheld thy son, thine only son from me." You see, Abraham did not withhold his son from God, and God could see Abraham's heart. I don't know that Abraham understood the prophetic ramifications of his statement in verse 8, but with our 20/20 hindsight, it doesn't seem likely that the choice of words were coincidence. God did indeed offer *himself* up as the sacrifice on the cross on this very same hill.

As we progress further into the tale, we see yet more similarities. Isaac, as a type of Christ, was a willing participant. Abraham binds him and puts him on the altar, but Abraham is well past a hundred years old, and Isaac is a strong young man. Had he not been willing, Abraham would not have been able to accomplish all that he did (Genesis 22:9–10). Likewise, Christ was a willing participant in his own death. They did not take his life from him; he freely gave it.

> Therefore doth my Father love me, because
> I lay down my life, that I might take it again.
> No man taketh it from me, but I lay it down of
> myself. I have power to lay it down, and I have

power to take it again. This commandment have
I received of my Father. (John 10:17–18)

As Abraham raised the knife to plunge it into his much-loved
son, God stopped him (Genesis 22:12). According to Jewish law in
Old Testament times, a man was considered dead from the moment
the death penalty was pronounced. God told Abraham what was
expected of him, and from that moment, Isaac was legally considered
dead for the entire journey to Mount Moriah. Three days later, Isaac
was given life back when his death sentence was rescinded with the
arrival of the ram. Just as Christ was the sacrifice, and three days later,
he rose from the dead. The story of Abraham's faith and obedience
allows us to see a model of the death of God's only Son, his three days
in the grave, and his resurrection.

Now our typology temporarily changes, and Isaac becomes a
type of believer saved from death by the death of another. The ram
caught in the thicket becomes a type of Christ. He was caught by his
horns in a thicket of Acacia, and our Lord wore a crown of thorns
from the Acacia at his crucifixion. "And Abraham went and took the
ram, and offered him up for a burnt offering in the stead of his son"
(Genesis 22:13). God gives Abraham a message regarding his seed
in verse 18. Abraham is told that "in thy seed shall all nations of the
earth be blessed." This is again a reference to the Messiah. Jesus was
the seed of Abraham, and he blessed all the nations of the earth, not
just the Jewish people, with his salvation message.

Could all of these similarities between the two lives, Isaac and
Jesus, be coincidence? I don't believe so. And it's not over yet. There
is as much meaning in what God doesn't say as there is in what he
does say. After all, much Jewish history is not recorded in the biblical record. How did God decide what his prophets would write and
what they should not write? He had them record everything we need
to know to help us identify the coming Messiah at both his first and
second comings and what we needed to know to build our faith and
help us to be conformed to the image of Christ. Isaac, as a type of
Christ, has symbolically died and been brought back from the dead
just as Christ literally died and rose from the dead at his first coming.

Now, Christ is not physically with us, so let's look further at Isaac's example and see if it gives us any more insight into our Lord.

Though we know Isaac came back down the mountain with Abraham, it is not recorded in the scriptures. Let's keep in mind that God's Word is precise and exact in what it doesn't say as well as in what it does. Isaac is not mentioned again in our text for a couple of chapters. He is conspicuously left out of the account of Abraham coming off of the mountain in Genesis 22:19, though we know he was there. In chapter 23, Sarah, Isaac's mother, dies and is buried, but Isaac is still absent from the narrative. Why?

To solve this mystery, let's look at what's happening when he does reappear on the scene. Abraham, the father, sent an unnamed servant to go get a bride for his son (Genesis 24:2–4). This unnamed servant finds her and brings her to Isaac. Likewise, the Father God has sent the Holy Spirit to bring a bride, the church, to his Son Jesus. Rebekah is a type of the bride of Christ, or the church, and the unnamed servant is a type of the Holy Spirit. Why is it significant that the servant of Genesis 24:5 is unnamed? Well, as a type of the Holy Spirit, the servant with no name received no glory for his deeds. The Holy Spirit also never draws attention to himself or desires to receive glory for his deeds. Rather, he testifies of Jesus Christ just as the unnamed servant of Abraham testifies to Rebekah of Isaac, the son.

> Howbeit when he, the Spirit of truth, is come, he will guide you into all truth: for he shall not speak of himself; but whatsoever he shall hear, that shall he speak: and he will shew you things to come. He shall glorify me: for he shall receive of mine, and shall shew it unto you. (John 16:13–14)

Isaac is not mentioned in the scriptures again until the unnamed servant meets him with his bride, Rebekah. Likewise, Christ is sitting at the right hand of the Father, and we shall not see him again until he catches away his bride to meet him in the air.

Some will say that the unnamed servant of Genesis 24:5 is not really unnamed because we "know" that it was probably Eliezer—Abraham's most trusted servant. Well, first off, we can suppose this to be true, but since the servant is not named in this passage of scripture, we don't know that with a certainty. If we go ahead and presume it was Eliezer who went in search of a bride for the son, it's still surprisingly consistent. The name Eliezer means "comforter," and in John 16:7, Christ calls the Holy Spirit the comforter. Again, the consistency of Scripture precludes the possibility that this is only a compilation of history written by multiple people. Only by the inspiration of God could such complexities be devoid of contradiction.

Moving forward through the Bible, Isaac had Jacob and Esau, twin boys. Esau's descendants became the Edomites or Jordanians of today. Esau lost his birthright and blessing to his younger brother, Jacob. Through these events, Jacob inherited the right to be in the hereditary line of the Messiah. Jacob's name was changed to Israel in Genesis 32:28. Jacob means "he who supplants (replaces)" or "he who tricks." Israel means "he who rules with God" or "he who struggles with God." I'd say Jacob's name change was a positive thing. Jacob's twelve sons became the twelve tribes of Israel. His first four sons were the sons of his first wife, Leah. They were, in birth order, Reuben, Simeon, Levi, and Judah. Since the oldest son is the son with the legal inheritance rights, why is the line of the kings and therefore the line of the Messiah through Judah and not through Reuben? Judah is, after all, fourth in line. Well, let's start with Reuben and look at each of Jacob's first three boys and find out why they lost the birthright to be in the lineage of our Lord.

In Genesis 49, we see the blessings that Jacob gave to each of his sons. The Old Testament blessings the fathers gave to their sons were more than simply a father's expression of love and wishes for their sons' lives. They were God-inspired prophecies of their future and their descendant's future (Genesis 49:1). In Genesis 49:3–4, Jacob begins with the blessing to Reuben, his firstborn and the one who should receive the right to rule. He begins by saying nice things about Reuben (verse 3). Verse 4 then goes on to say, "Unstable as water, thou shalt not excel; because thou wentest up to thy father's bed; then defiledst thou it; he went up to my couch." What is Jacob referring to? Reuben lost his legal position as first son because he slept with Jacob's handmaid, Bilhah (Genesis 35:22). Bilhah was the mother of Dan and Naphtali and therefore Reuben's stepmother. So Reuben lost his standing.

This would put Simeon in the position of the firstborn. The Messiah should be the Lion of the tribe of Simeon then, but he's not. Looking at the blessing for Simeon in Genesis 49:5–7, we see that Simeon and Levi receive their blessings together as though they are one.

> Simeon and Levi are brethren, instruments of cruelty and in their habitations. O my soul, come not thou into their secret; unto their assembly, mine honor, be not thou united: for in their anger they slew a man, and in their self-will they digged down a wall. Cursed be their anger, for it was fierce; and their wrath, for it was cruel: I will divide them in Jacob, and scatter them in Israel.

Jacob was referring to the slaughter of the Hivites. In Genesis 34, we see a story that reads like a novel. Jacob's daughter Dinah was defiled by Shechem—a Hivite prince who decided he must have her for his own. Dinah is the full sister of Simeon and Levi, the daughter of Leah. When Shechem and his father approached Jacob and his sons to ask for Dinah's hand in marriage, the sons of Jacob tricked them (Genesis 34:13). They told Shechem that he could marry Dinah but only on the condition that all of the men of their tribe were circumcised. On the third day, when all of the men of the city were very sore, Simeon and Levi fell upon the city with their swords and killed all of the males, including Shechem and his father, and then they freed their sister. They then took, as the spoils of war, all of their animals, women, and children to have for their own. This event is the "cruelty" and "anger" Jacob is referring to in Genesis 49:5–7, and it was this event that caused Simeon and Levi to be disenfranchised of their birthright to become the kingly line.

The next in line then would be Judah. Genesis 49:8–12 shows the prophecy regarding Judah, and a fascinating prophecy it is too. He starts out explaining how Judah's brothers will bow down before him, showing his position of power. In verse 9, he calls Judah a "lion's whelp," and Christ is called the Lion of the tribe of Judah. Verse 10 says, "The scepter shall not depart from Judah…" indicating that the kingly line and, therefore, the line of the Messiah shall be from this tribe. Verse 11 prophecies of the First Coming of Christ culminating with his Crucifixion. "Binding his foal unto the vine, and his ass's colt unto the choice vine; he washed his garments in wine, and his clothes in the blood of grapes." Verse 12 refers to his Second Coming. So Judah is given the blessing that should've been reserved for the eldest child, even though he was fourth in line.

Why then was Israel's first king, Saul, a Benjamite? Why wasn't he from the tribe of Judah since he was anointed by God to be king? Why this apparent inconsistency?

The solution to this problem is found in Genesis 33. Judah, this fourth son of Jacob, had a son named Er. Er married a Canaanite woman named Tamar (Genesis 38:6). Er was so wicked that God "slew him" in verse 7 of Genesis 38. Under Levitical law, when a woman lost a husband, the next of kin was obligated to marry her and give her offspring in the name of her deceased husband, if she had none (Deuteronomy 25:5). This made Onan, the next eldest brother, in line to marry Tamar. However, Onan wasn't interested in producing an heir for his brother, and he spilled his seed on the ground thus refusing his obligation under the law (Genesis 38:9). God then slew him also. This left Judah's youngest and now only son, Shelah. Shelah was too young at this time to produce an offspring, so Judah told Tamar to go back to her father's home and live there until Shelah was old enough to marry. He would then call for her, and Shelah would marry her and fulfill the obligation. Judah, however, had decided that Tamar was cursed since everybody she married died, and he was afraid to let Shelah marry her for fear that he too would die. So when Shelah was old enough to marry, he did not send for Tamar. Well, small towns being what they are, Tamar heard of this deception and set out to trick Judah into fulfilling this obligation.

She found out Judah's schedule, dressed as a harlot, and waited for him on the street corner (Genesis 38:18).

Judah came into town, and she caught his eye. He propositioned her, not realizing who she truly was. He offered her a kid from his flock as payment. He didn't happen to have the kid with him, so they made an arrangement that he would give her his signet right, bracelet, and staff as collateral, and tomorrow, his servants would bring the kid and retrieve his belongings. The business arrangement was agreed upon. The next day, however, when the servants arrive to trade the kid for the valued possessions, Tamar is nowhere to be found. None of the locals know of any prostitute that sits on that street corner peddling her wares. So Judah is just out of luck.

Time went on and, as small towns are, the gossip was flying, and word reached Judah's ear that his daughter-in-law, his still *unmarried* daughter-in-law, was pregnant. Judah demanded that she be brought before him and killed. She was brought before him and handed him his signet ring, bracelet, and staff. That must've been a little humbling, perhaps a bit of an eye-opener for Judah. Genesis 38:26 says, "And Judah acknowledged them, and said, She hath been more righteous than I because that I gave her not to Shelah my son. And he knew her again no more." So Tamar had twins. They were Pharez and Zarah. Pharez, as the oldest, would carry on the kingly line. However, there is a law that limits children born out of wedlock. According to the Levitical law, a child born out of wedlock cannot enter into the congregation (or sit on the throne of the messianic line) for ten generations (Deuteronomy 23:2).

A careful check for the messianic genealogy of both Matthew 1 and Ruth 4 reveals that David, from the tribe of Judah, was the tenth in line, and the curse of pharez ended with his anointing as king of Israel. You see, while the Jews were demanding a king, Jesse could not be king because he was still under the curse. Saul, from the tribe of Benjamin, then, was anointed king. David was his successor because he was from the royal tribe of Judah and was the first one not under the curse. God desired them to wait for his timing, but Israel demanded a king before David was ready to be the first king. Thus, God gave them Saul.

"And the scepter shall not depart from Judah, nor a law giver from between his feet until Shiloh come, and unto him shall the gathering of the people be" (Genesis 49:10). Shiloh means "rest or tranquility" and is a reference to Christ. Jesus said, "Come unto me all ye that labor and are heavy laden, and I will give you rest" (Matthew 11:28). Shiloh was a city located north of Jerusalem where the tabernacle was located when the Israelites first entered into the promised land in 1452 BC. It *rested* there until Solomon's Temple was completed in about 950 BC. The presence of God *rested* in the tabernacle and, later, the temple; our salvation *rests* in Christ because of his finished work on the cross. And his peace *rests* in us because we are the temple of the living God.

Looking at Jacob's twelve sons again, let's focus a moment on Benjamin. The last two sons Jacob had were Joseph and Benjamin. They were the only two sons born to Jacob's beloved wife, Rachel and, definitely, his favorites. Rachel died in childbirth when Benjamin was born. Before her death, Rachel named the child Benoni, which in Hebrew means "son of sorrow" (Genesis 35:18). Benoni was a foreshadowing of the First Coming of Christ, for Christ was a son of sorrow (Isaiah 53:3; Psalm 22:6). After Rachel's death, Jacob changed Benoni's name to Benjamin or "son of my right hand" (Genesis 35:18). Christ is now seated at the right hand of God the Father (Psalm 110:1; Matthew 22:44; Hebrews 1:13).

To see the symbolism of this second version of Benjamin's name played out, we'll do a quick recap of the story of Benjamin's only full brother, Joseph. Joseph, the dreamer of dreams, was not well-liked by his jealous brothers. Joseph was a little cocky and a bit of a bragger, no doubt worsened by his father's favoritism. After Joseph received the special coat from his father, his brothers sold him into slavery (Genesis 37). We look forward twenty years, and we see Joseph has risen to a very high position in the Egyptian government (Genesis 39). The land is in terrible drought, and there is widespread famine, and Joseph's brothers (except Benjamin) travel to Egypt to purchase food. They don't recognize Joseph as their brother; after all, it has been twenty years, and he was only a teenager then. Now, he's a man, dressed as a prince, and speaking another language. He, however, recognizes them. He wants to see his little brother, and he wants to test the hearts of his big brothers to see if they have changed their wicked ways. Joseph, without revealing his identity, binds up his brother Simeon and imprisons him. He's to remain bound and imprisoned until the other brothers return to Egypt with Benjamin.

There's typology if we look a little deeper. Simeon's name means "hearing" or "harkening." Israel has long been accused by her ancient prophets of being dull of hearing (Isaiah 28:11–12, 65:12). Simeon, locked up in his Egyptian prison, represents Israel with her hearing locked up and not functioning. Egypt represents the world. Israel became imprisoned in the world when the Diaspora occurred: the dispersion of the Jews taken out of their land during their occupation and scattered all over the world. They, like Simeon, will remain hard of hearing and dispersed among the nations until they receive their Messiah until the Son of the Father's right hand comes to save them and release them from their prison. Benjamin's coming to Egypt to free his brother's "hearing" from the chains of bondage in the prison of the world represents Christ's Second Coming.

There is a New Testament connection to Simeon's name and holding the same theme. In Luke 2:22–28, Mary and Joseph brought Jesus to the temple for the baby Jesus's dedication. A man named Simeon was present in the temple at the time. Simeon was very old, and God had promised him that he would not see death until he beheld the promised Messiah. Luke 2:34–35 says, "And Simeon blessed them, and said unto Mary his mother, behold, this child is set for the fall and rising again for many in Israel; and for a sign which shall be spoken against." Simeon, whose name means "hearing," is giving a prophecy related to Israel's hearing and not hearing. It is Israel's dullness of hearing that caused her to reject the Messiah. Rejection of the Messiah caused many to fall in Israel (John 1:11). According to Hosea 5:15–6:3, Israel will acknowledge him and call out for him, and he will deliver them, thus creating the "rising again." Simeon's words were definitely prophetic.

Moses also was a walking example of a literal person experiencing literal events while God uses those events to prophecy in a symbolic manner of the coming of Christ. One of my favorite examples of this is Moses and the rock. Moses had led the children of Israel into the wilderness, and there was no water. The people were complaining to Moses and demanding he provide water for them. The Lord came to Moses in Exodus 17 and told him to strike the rock. Moses struck the rock, and water spewed forth, and the children of Israel drank their fill. Later, in Numbers 20, this same situation was occurring again. Again, there was no water in the dessert. Again, the Israelites were complaining and demanding of Moses. Moses went to the Lord again, and in verse 8, the Lord tells Moses to speak to the rock. Moses got angry at the lack of faith the children of Israel expressed, and he struck the rock in his anger instead of speaking to it as God had commanded him. Water came forth, but Moses got put in the penalty box. God told him, in verse 12, that because he did not believe and obey, he would not be allowed to enter into the promised land.

This seems like an awfully harsh punishment for one moment of weakness, especially for a man of God of this caliber—a man who believed God would perform miraculous plagues, part the Red Sea, and had led the children of Israel across the wilderness where their food was supplied daily by the hand of God. But Moses had messed with the model. God wanted his Word and the events in it to testify of Christ's coming, and Moses messed up the model God was setting up. Christ is the rock. "Jesus Christ himself being the chief corner stone" (Ephesians 2:20 and also in Luke 20:17). "What is this then that is written, the stone which the builders rejected, the same is become the head of the corner?" (Jesus was quoting Psalm 118:22). The final and most plain scripture to support this is 1 Corinthians 10:4: "And did all drink the same spiritual drink; for they drank of that spiritual Rock that followed them: and that Rock was Christ." So Jesus is the rock, and the first time he comes, he comes to be stricken. The first time Moses was told to smite the rock. The second time Jesus comes, he comes in the power of his Word—the second time Moses was told to speak to the rock. You see, Moses messed up the model God was trying to put in his Word for future generations to have a foreshadowing of Christ's two comings, and that's why Moses paid such a harsh penalty for his disobedience.

A similar theme of the rock is seen in Exodus 33. Moses wanted to see the Lord and his glory. God told him,

> And he said, thou canst not see my face: for there shall no man see me and live. And the Lord said, behold, there is a place by me, and thou shalt stand upon a rock: and it shall come to pass, while my glory passeth by, that I will put thee in a clift of the rock, and will cover thee with my hand while I pass by: And I will take away mine hand, and thou shalt see my back parts: but my face shall not be seen.

We too are only safe from the overwhelming glory of God if we hide in the cleft of the rock—that rock being Jesus. This is the only way we can even see a glimpse of the Father by hiding in the safety of the Son. I thank God daily for giving me the opportunity!

Prophecy in the Bible, whether it be in words, types, or symbols, is incredibly consistent. What is the primary purpose of prophecy? Is it edification of the individual? No, though it does edify. Is it for the building of faith for the body of Christ? No, though it does build faith. Is it to glorify the prophet and make him famous? Certainly not, though these prophets have become very famous. Revelation 19:10 tells us, "For the testimony of Jesus is the spirit of prophecy." That's the primary purpose of prophecy—to testify of Jesus. Through that, we do build faith and receive edification, and we give glory only to God.

In the Old Testament, the testimony of Jesus, and therefore prophecy, had to be future-telling. In the New Testament, the testimony of Jesus's Second Coming was still future-telling and, therefore, so was prophecy. Also, in the New Testament, the testimony of Jesus's First Coming was present and, therefore, forthtelling, though it is still prophecy. The entire purpose of the prophecies was to testify of Jesus before, during, and after his coming. The Bible is so riddled with prophetic words, fulfilled to the jot and tittle, some spelled out for us and many in riddle form.

I am convinced we will spend a lifetime finding them and yet never finding them all—further testimony to the inspiration in the Word of God. So let us all go out and testify of our Lord today. Go testify of Jesus Christ, from the Old and New Testaments, and keep the spirit of prophecy.

CHAPTER 5

Tabernacle

Probably one of the most prominent examples of Christ in the Old Testament is the model of the tabernacle. The study of this dwelling place of God certainly reveals God's use of symbolism and models as a foreshadowing of the coming of his Son. There is a significant amount of space in the scriptures devoted to describing the details and specifications of the Tabernacle thus emphasizing the importance of this structure. Nothing is in the Bible without reason; there are no accidents, so perhaps, we should look closer at these descriptions and begin to analyze the symbolism. It's important that our symbols be consistent throughout the Bible as God has proven over and over again in his Word that he is consistent. When we follow this basic principle of consistency, and we analyze every aspect of God's Old Testament dwelling place, we see that every facet is a picture of Christ. We're going to begin on the outside and journey all the way to the holy of holies, analyzing each aspect as we go.

An overview of the Israelite's camp and their tabernacle reveals already a prophecy of the coming of our Lord. We're going to consult the book of Numbers chapters 2 and 3. These two chapters are devoted to a very specific description of where the tribes are to camp. Of course, their camp was on the move, which is why the tabernacle was a tent. When the Lord wanted them to move, the Shekinah glory of the Lord lifted and led the people in the form of fire by night and a cloud by day. When they settled, they were told exactly where to camp and with whom. Why would God give such specific instruction?

First of all, the tabernacle was to be the center of the camp. It was to be carried, set up, and cared for by the Levites. Next, Numbers chapter 2 describes the tribes that were to camp on the east side of the tabernacle. It specifies that the tribe of Judah, with 74,600 men counted, the tribe of Issachar, with 54,500 men, and Zebulun, with 57,400 men, would all camp to the east of God's dwelling place. This is a total of 186,400 men to the east. It then describes the camps that were to camp to the south. They are as follows: Reuben with 46,500 men, Simeon with 59,300 men, and Gad with 45,650 men, totaling 151,450 men. To the west would be the following tribes: Ephraim with 40,500 men, Manasseh with 32,300 men, and Benjamin with 35,400 men for a total of 108,100 men. Finally, to the north are Dan with 62,700 men, Asher with 41,500, and Naphtali with 53,400 men, totaling 157,600 in these three tribes.

These specific directions seem pointless at first glance and possibly even boring to read. After all, we're not camping around the tabernacle. And yet, the Bible is written for future generations and therefore contains a message for us. If these were simply directions only for those that lived during that time period and had no bearing on our lives, then I'm sure God would've told them only and not bothered to have it written in his Word. To help us see the incredible prophecy hidden in these camping instructions, let's draw a picture of what our camping Israelites would have looked like when settled in their proper places.

The first thing I notice is that the groups camping on the north and south have similar numbers of people. I then notice that the tribes camping to the west have the fewest number, and those camping to the east have the most people. Though the Israelites would not have been able to observe their overview from within the camp, their enemies looking down on their camp from the surrounding hills would've had an interesting view, as did God looking down upon his people. They would've all seen the following:

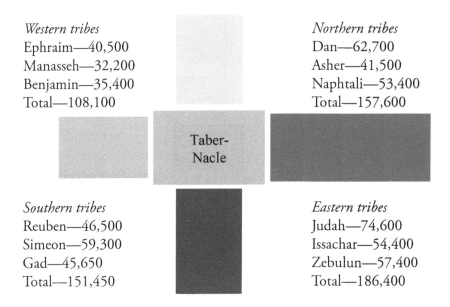

Western tribes
Ephraim—40,500
Manasseh—32,200
Benjamin—35,400
Total—108,100

Northern tribes
Dan—62,700
Asher—41,500
Naphtali—53,400
Total—157,600

Taber-
Nacle

Southern tribes
Reuben—46,500
Simeon—59,300
Gad—45,650
Total—151,450

Eastern tribes
Judah—74,600
Issachar—54,400
Zebulun—57,400
Total—186,400

When God gets specific, it's intentional. It's not an accident that they were camped in the shape of a cross; it's prophetic. They didn't understand the significance; after all, the method of crucifying criminals had not yet been invented. But we now see, through our 20/20 hindsight, that God was giving a prophecy of his Son's death on the cross. Through Christ's death and resurrection, we have access to the throne of the living God, and through the Tabernacle in the Old Testament, the Israelites had access to the Shekinah glory of God.

We will now examine the description of the tabernacle itself. The following specifics are found in Exodus 24–27 and Exodus 37–38. In Exodus 25:8–9, we see God telling Moses, "And let them make me a sanctuary; that I may dwell among them. According to all that I show thee, after the pattern of the tabernacle, and the pattern of all the instruments thereof, even so shall ye make it." It then gives some descriptions and goes on to say, "And look that thou make them after the pattern, which was showed thee in the mount" (Exodus 25:40). So God, in addition to the Ten Commandments, gave Moses a pattern of the tabernacle while he was up on Mount Sinai. It is a pattern that modeled the tabernacle that's in heaven.

The first thing we will note is that there is only one gate. This is not an accident as there is only one way to God. Jesus said in John 14:6, "Jesus saith unto him, I am the way the truth, and the life; no man cometh unto the Father, but by me." The gate is to the east, as were the entrance to the garden of Eden and the entrance to the heavenly tabernacle in the heavens. The east is the direction of the rising of the sun, and our spiritual existence relies upon the rising of the Son and our ability to access God.

The next thing I notice about the gate is the fact that the tribe Judah is one of the tribes to the east of the gate. You must pass through the tribe of Judah in order to enter the tabernacle and therefore access the presence of God. Christ, of course, is the Lion of the tribe of Judah, and in order to access God, we must go through Christ.

The colors are the next thing I notice while looking at the tabernacle from the outside. The walls were made of wooden posts with a cap and hook of silver set into a brass base and then had white linen walls stretched around the outer court. Over the gate were the following colors: blue, red, white, and purple. When looking at the tabernacle of God, the white linen signifies purity; isn't that what we need to seek in order to access the throne of God? Isn't Christ purity incarnate—the spotless lamb, the sinless man? Red symbolizes the blood; purple is for kings, and blue is the color of the heavens. Each color is an aspect of God.

The metals also hold symbolic meaning. Brass represents judgment, always in the Scripture. The staff that Moses used that saved the Israelites in Numbers 21:8–9 had a brass serpent on it. The serpent represented sin; the brass represented judgment, thus the staff represented sin being judged. John tells us that the brass serpent was a foreshadowing of Christ in John 3:14, and while we are bothered by the idea that Christ would be represented by a serpent, we must remember that Christ became our sin.

> God made him who had no sin to be sin for us, so that in him we might become the righteousness of God. (2 Corinthians 5:21)

The silver represents atonement or redemption (Leviticus). Gold represents God and King, both of which describe our Lord. The white walls have silver rings sewn into them which hang on the silver hooks attached to the silver caps of the poles. The foundation of the poles are the brass sockets.

With that foundation, we again look at the fence surrounding the Court of the Gentiles or outer court of the tabernacle. We see a white linen fence hung on the silver hooks and rings of the posts whose foundation is a brass socket. Our purity hangs on our redemption; the foundation of that redemption is judgment. Furthermore, there were sixty posts, each topped with 1/2 shekel of silver, making a total of thirty pieces of silver—the same price paid for Christ by the Jewish priests. Coincidence? Impossible.

We are now ready to enter in through the gate and into the outer court. It is interesting to note that the gold, silver, and brass that we see in the construction of the tabernacle were all gifts from the Egyptians when the Israelites were ready to leave Egypt. Remember, they were slaves and had no wealth of their own, but after the final plague wherein the eldest of each family died, the Egyptians were so glad to get rid of the Israelites that they gave them gifts. One day, they were poor slaves; the next day, they were wealthy and free. God truly does provide.

In the outer court, we see two pieces of furniture. The first thing we would see as we entered through the gate was the altar of sacrifice. This was a large box that measure five cubits by five cubits by three cubits high. A cubit is approximately nineteen inches, so this altar measured just under eight square foot. It was completely covered in brass and had a grate in the bottom and rings on the corners to put the staves through for transportation purposes.

Having this altar just inside the gate, the first thing you see as you enter the outer court must've been quite an unpleasant sight. There must be a sacrifice made to cover the sin, so God cannot see the sin when he looks upon us, and this act was done right inside the gate of the tabernacle's outer court. The sacrifice was to be a clean animal, according to what the family could afford. Goats, lambs, doves and bullocks are all examples of animals that were brought to this altar to be sacrificed. It was not a pretty sight, and I'm sure the smell of blood was overwhelming at times, but then our sin is not a pretty sight in the eyes of God and a stench in his nostrils. Sin must be judged, but again, this altar is but a foreshadowing of a more perfect plan. The blood of bulls and goats could only cover the sin. The blood of the Lamb of God, the final sacrifice, is the ultimate payment of our sins since his blood doesn't cover our sins but washes them away. In John 19:30, Christ said, "It is finished," and he died. The altar of sacrifice is a model of Christ's first coming. John 1:29 says, "The next day John seeth Jesus coming unto him, and saith, behold the Lamb of God which taketh away the sin of the world."

The only other piece of furniture in the outer court is the brazen laver. This is an interesting piece of furniture. It is placed just outside the gate into the building itself and is filled with water for ceremonial washing. It is also made from brass, representing judgment. You will notice that brass is the only metal represented in the outer court because the first step to accessing God is the judgment required for our sins. But the brazen laver is not made from just any old brass; it is made from the polished brass mirrors of the Egyptians. Remember, they didn't have glass mirrors, so they used polished brass, and these were melted down to create the brazen laver.

This is a great representation showing the need for humility before we may enter into God's presence. Christ gave the sacrifice, but before we can wash ourselves clean, we must look honestly upon ourselves and confess our inability to achieve God's standards. We are to wash ourselves in the water, and again, this is Christ. Ephesians 5:26 says, "That he might sanctify and cleanse it [the church] with the washing of the water by the word."

The ceremonial cleansing in the brazen laver is representative of washing of our sins with Christ, and this takes humility; we must see ourselves as God sees us. This is the reason for baptism as well. It symbolizes our spiritual death and rebirth through the washing of the water which is Christ, the Word. In John 3:5, Jesus said, "Verily, verily, I say unto thee, except a man be born of water and of the Spirit, he cannot enter into the Kingdom of God." He doesn't mean that we must be baptized to be saved. If that were true, he would not have told the thief on the cross that he would see him today in para-dise. The thief on the cross recognized Christ for who he was but was not baptized. And yet he went to paradise with the Lord. To be born of the water is the reality that the baptism symbolizes. It is the same thing that is symbolized by the washing of the priests at the brazen laver. It's the washing of the Word. We need to immerse ourselves in God's Word. That's how we get to know and have a relationship with Christ: by getting into his Word. The more we know the Word, the more we know Christ; he is, after all, the Word.

> In the beginning was the Word, and the Word was with God, and the Word was God. (John 1:1)

Our salvation experience is right here in the outer court of the tabernacle. Christ has already been sacrificed. The next step then is to look humbly upon myself through the mirror of judgment and recognize that I am a sinner, and I cannot reach God's standard. I then wash myself in the living water, and Christ will cleanse me from my sin. Then and only then, I may begin to enter into the presence of the living God. And when Christ died, according to John 19:34, "one of the soldiers with a spear pierced his side, and forthwith came there out blood and water"—the same two ingredients found in the outer court of the tabernacle.

Now, before we actually enter the building, I want to look at the construction of the tabernacle building as seen from the outside. The tabernacle itself was constructed of forty-eight boards, all coated in gold. They were assembled by running five rows of poles, also coated in gold, through rings (you guessed it, coated in gold) that were attached to the outside of the boards. Each board also had two tenons on the bottom of the board, which were placed in two sock-ets/bases made of pure silver. The east wall is the entrance, of course, and has no boards, just five posts. The west wall (back wall) is made up of six boards, forty boards for the north and south walls, and two boards at the back corners strengthening that potential weak spot, making the total of forty-eight boards (Exodus 36:20–30) The gate, similar to the gate into the outer court, has the same colors above it: white, blue, purple, and red.

These forty-eight boards just happen to be the same number as the number of cities given to the tribe of Levi (Numbers 35). When the twelve tribes were given land as an inheritance, the tribe of Levi received no land; God told them *he* was their inheritance. The reason for this is that, once they reach the promised land, the Levites need to be located in each of the tribal areas so that they could minister to the spiritual needs of the people. They did, however, receive forty-eight cities interspersed throughout the twelve other tribes. These forty-eight cities are represented by the forty-eight boards that make up the tabernacle.

Just as there are six boards at the back of the tabernacle, six of these forty-eight cities were cities of refuge—three on one side of the Jordan River, three on the other side of the Jordan River. The cities of refuge operated in the following manner: if you inadvertently killed someone through negligence or carelessness, not intentionally (today, we would call it manslaughter), the family of the victim had the legal right to come find you and kill you. An eye for an eye was the law. All murdered victims had this avenue for justice. But assuming the "murder" was not intentional and was a manslaughter case, the guilty party had the right to flee to the nearest city of refuge. The family of the victim could not enter the city to pursue you, the murderer, but you would only be protected within the boundaries of the city. In a sense, you were imprisoned in that city. Now, your sentence would be up only when the high priest died. The high priest was located in Jerusalem and not in one of the cities of refuge, so he was not endangered by this murderer. As soon as the high priest died, you were free to leave the city and go where you wanted, and the family of the victim no longer had the legal right to kill you; you had served your time.

Within the tabernacle, those west six boards at the backside of the building represented the six cities of refuge the Levites inherited. In order to get to the cities of refuge on the back wall of the tabernacle, you had to go through the outer court, through the holy place (the first room in the building), through the veil, and through the holy of holies which is where the presence of God rests. So you had to take the road of salvation to access the backboards.

Of course, the cities of refuge, also, are simply models or representations of Christ. Through our sin, we have inadvertently killed the Lord, an innocent man. Our sin nailed him to the cross, though we did not go out to intentionally kill him; we are guilty of manslaughter. Christ himself declared it to be manslaughter, not murder. He said, "Father forgive them for they *know not what they* do" (Luke 23:34). God, the next of kin to the victim, then has the legal right to find us and kill us to enact judgment for the death of his Son. But by fleeing to Christ, our city of refuge, he will wash away our sin and keep us from the wrath we deserve. But the beauty of it all is that Christ is also our High Priest, and at his death, we were then free from our obligations to be "imprisoned" within the city of refuge; our debt is completely forgiven. He paid it in full. At the moment of his death, we were simultaneously guilty and innocent. We are set free. What a fabulous model God has given us to help us understand the incredible message of his Son.

Back in the tabernacle building, we see that the metals are also significant, and from here on are mostly gold. The boards are covered in gold; the furnishings in the tabernacle itself are gold, and even the accessories are gold: rings, dishes, etc. Gold represents deity or royalty. It shows where God resides within the walls. The foundation of the building itself, the bases that the boards are placed in, are solid silver. Silver represents atonement for sins, and surely, the entire foundation of having access to God is the atonement for our sins. Without it, we could not approach the Almighty without sudden destruction coming upon us. God hates sin. He loves the sinner and therefore provides a way for us to atone for our sins so that we may have access to him without judgment falling upon us.

The building had a tentlike covering over it, actually in four separate layers. The first layer was made of strips of the same four colors sewn together and had cherubim embroidered onto the covering so that they would be looking down into the building. This must have been very beautiful but was only seen from the inside. The next layer was of goat's hair and the next of lamb's skins dyed red. The final covering, which is the only one seen from the outside, is made of "sea cows" (NIV).

Looking at the tent coverings starting from the inside out, the first covering was of linen, purple, red, and blue stitched together embroidered with cherubim and was the most beautiful. Cherubim are a "super angel" of which there are two types mentioned in the Bible. The other super angels are Seraphim, and these two types of angels are the only ones with wings. Angels, as a rule, do not have wings, and *none* of them are women. The cherubim and seraphim do, however, have wings. They serve different purposes, and I would like you to note that there are no Seraphim in the tabernacle. Seraphim have the job of judging sin, and once you have entered the tabernacle proper, the judgment of your sin has already been accomplished through the sacrifice and washing in the water. The job of the cherubim is to guard the throne of God. So these cherubim are embroidered into the first covering and looking down into the very presence of God—to guard the throne. Satan too was a cherubim; how treacherous it was to have the job of guarding the throne and instead attempt to usurp it.

This first covering was made in ten individual strips sewn together into two separate sections of five strips in each. The two sections were then attached with hooks and rings. This construction is a perfect representation of the Ten Commandments. These Ten Commandments are broken down by the Lord into two commandments. Jesus said unto them, "Thou shalt love the Lord thy god with all thy heart, and with all thy soul, and with all thy mind. This is the first and great commandment. And the second is like unto it, Thou shalt love thy neighbor as thyself. On these two commandments hang all the law and the prophets" (Matthew 22:36–40).

The next two coverings are sacrificial animals: goats and lambs. The outside covering is said to be "sea cow" in the NIV or "badger" in the King James. Badger is not the correct translation, and it is said that the reason it was translated badger is because they didn't know what a sea cow was, and they translated the color rather than the animal. It was a blackish bluish color, similar to the coloring of a badger. The most likely definition of a sea cow is the dugong that lives in the

Red Sea. They are kind of like a manatee or a vegetarian seal. They are a mammal but live in the water. Their hide is thick, waterproof, and not particularly attractive. Imagine the beauty of this gold building, filled with gold furnishings, the beauty of the first tent covering, and it's all hidden by this bland, unattractive dugong skin. Much like Christ himself. He is the Son of God, God incarnate, the Lily of the Valley, Lion of the tribe of Judah, Counselor, Almighty God, Prince of Peace, long awaited Messiah, and so much more. I could go on and on, and yet in Isaiah 53:2, it is said of Christ, "For he shall grow up before him as a tender plant, and as a root out of a dry ground: he hath no form nor comeliness; and when we shall see him, there is no beauty that we should desire him." God did not want people to seek after Christ because of his beauty, and likewise, he disguised the beauty of his tabernacle with the plain, unremarkable but practical skin of the dugong.

We will now enter the tabernacle proper and discuss the furnishings we find there. Against the right or north wall is the table of showbread. This table is coated completely in gold with gold rings on the corners to hold the gold coated staves that were used to transport. It holds on it twelve loaves of unleavened bread. Leaven, of course, represents sin, so there can be no leaven in the tabernacle of God and no sin in the presence of the Almighty. The twelve loaves represent the twelve tribes of Israel. They are also representative of Christ as he is said to be the Bread of Life.

> And Jesus said unto them, I am the bread
> of life: he that cometh to me shall never hunger;
> and he that believeth on me shall never thirst.
> (John 6:35)

On the south or left wall stands a most impressive lampstand. It is a seven-branch menorah that is pounded out of one continuous piece of gold. It is solid gold, not pieced together, because its continuity represents the continuity of God. The seven branches represent completeness, as the number seven is the number of completion. On the end of each of the branches sets a bowl that holds oil and a wick. This too represents Christ.

> Then spake Jesus again unto them, saying, I am the light of the world: he that followeth me shall not walk in darkness, but shall have the light of life. (John 8:12)

The lampstand is a complicated piece of furniture and requires some additional analysis. It is the light that lights the darkness but not by itself. The oil in each of the seven bowls represents the Holy Spirit, and the flame itself is the actual light that we are to reflect, meaning Christ. But what of the stand?

During the Old Testament times, the time of Israel and Old Testament saints, the menorah represented the tribe of Levi. The twelve loaves on the table of showbread are for each of the twelve tribes, but there are thirteen tribes. The menorah represents that thirteenth tribe. Out of Jacob's twelve sons, Joseph got a double portion, giving his twin sons each a tribe, Ephraim and Manasseh, and thus making thirteen tribes. We see all thirteen are present during the millennium (Ezekiel 48). The tribe of Levi was to be the witness to those around. The menorah has twenty-one almond buds on it, and Aaron's rod that budded in Numbers 17 budded with almond buds, showing which tribe God had chosen to be his mouthpiece.

During the age of the church, it is not the tribe of Levi that God is using for his mouthpiece but rather the Church. We are to be the light to the world; therefore, the menorah represents the church which holds the Holy Spirit and reflects the light of Christ. Revelation 1:20 tells us that the seven branches of the candlestick are the seven churches.

The last piece of furniture in this room is the altar of incense. Don't get it confused with the altar of sacrifice, which is in the outer court. The altar of incense is right in front of the veil that separates this room from the back room—the holy of holies. We are in the holy place now, which takes up about two-thirds of the space in the building. This altar that would stand straight ahead if we stood in the door is covered completely in gold. It is beautiful just as all of the furnishings in the building are. This is where the priests offer up prayers for the people. They took coals from the altar of sacrifice—coals that had the blood of the sacrifice on them and brought them into place on the altar of incense where they used these coals to burn incense. Incense represents the prayers of the people going up to God, and the Jews had to send up their prayers through their mediator: the priest. The priest made intercession for the people at the altar of incense. But today, Christ makes intercession for us. Hebrews 7:25 says, "Wherefore he is able to save them to the uttermost that come unto God by him, seeing he ever liveth to make intercession for them."

Directly past this piece of furniture is the veil that separates the holy place from the holy of holies. The veil was made of white linen, representing purity, with Cheribum embroidered in purple, red, and blue. God's glory rests in the holy of holies, and the people could not be directly in God's presence except once a year on the Day of Atonement or Yom Kippur. Even then, only the high priest could enter the holy of holies to sprinkle the blood of the sacrifice on the mercy seat of God. If the rules for entering this place were broken, the person who entered was struck dead. However, in order to approach the throne of God, you had to pass through the veil. Even this veil is a representative of our Lord. Hebrews 10:20 says, "By a new and living way which he has consecrated through the veil, that is to say, his flesh." So the veil is Christ's flesh which was torn that we might enter boldly the holy of holies and approach the throne of the living God. "And, behold, the veil of the temple was rent in twain from the top to the bottom" (Matthew 27:51). This event that occurred at the death of Jesus signifies the direction of the damage of the veil. Man did not rip it; the tear began at the top. God reached out to man by giving his son to be "rent" or torn. And he was.

The posts in the tabernacle that hold up this veil were four posts. You will remember that at the entrance to the building, there were five posts, and now at the entrance to this room, there are only four. The reason for this is found in symbolisms. The first five posts represent the five books of the Law written by Moses: Genesis, Exodus, Leviticus, Numbers, and Deuteronomy. You cannot even enter into the building if you do not go through the Law. Christ said, "Think not that I am come to destroy the law, or the prophets: I am not come to destroy, but to fulfill" (Matthew 5:17). The Law was just and fair but not complete because it did not provide for redemption. So then came the Messiah. In order to enter into the holiest room, the holy of holies, you had to go through the four posts or the four Gospels: Matthew, Mark, Luke, and John. These posts represent the gospels and, therefore, the good news. This doesn't mean we are bound by the Law because we are set free with God's grace. But the Law teaches us that we are sinners and incapable of saving ourselves. The Law was impossible for men to keep thus the necessity for grace. But through the Law, man recognizes his need for Christ, and this is humbling. This humility is necessary for salvation. After all, if I can do it myself, why would I come to God?

These four posts hold up the veil that separated the holy place from the holy of holies. This veil was beautiful, was made of blue, purple, red, and fine linen with cherubim on it (Exodus 26:31). Once a year, the high priest would enter into the holy of holies to place the blood of the sacrifice on the mercy seat of the ark of the covenant. He was timid to do this and even had a rope tied to his ankle in case he was struck dead while in there. No one else was permitted to enter, and on no other day was the high priest allowed in but only on the Day of Atonement. Also, if the priest did not prepare himself properly, God could strike him dead, hence the rope. If he were struck dead while in the holy of holies, the other priests could drag him out by the rope around his ankle. At the death of Christ, the veil was torn from top to bottom (Matthew 27:51). God himself tore the veil as he reached out to man at the death of his son. Hebrews 10:20 tells us that the veil symbolizes the flesh of Christ, which was torn for us. With the veil torn, we may enter the presence of God ourselves anytime we desire, and we need not be timid as we approach.

Let us therefore come *boldly* unto the throne
of grace that we may obtain mercy and find grace
to help in time of need. (Hebrews 5:16)

The holy of holies is the location where you are truly standing in the presence of the Almighty. It has but one single piece of furniture in this room. There is no chair in the holy of holies because the work was not yet finished. Now, however, Christ sits at the right hand of the Father because the work is complete.

The ark of the covenant was the only piece housed in this room. It was made of Shittim wood, also known as acacia wood. Wood symbolizes man, and this wood symbolizes Christ as Man. It was completely covered in gold, which represents royalty and deity, thus it is Christ as God. Christ is both man and God just as the ark was both wood and gold. Acacia wood was a thorny wood just as the wood that the ram caught his thorns in when he became the replacement sacrifice for Isaac. It also was the type of wood that made up the crown of thorns Christ wore on the cross when he became the replacement sacrifice for us. This ark had for its lid the mercy seat. This was made of gold and had two cherubim on it facing each other with their wings touching above the "seat." This was where the high priest, on the Day of Atonement, sprinkled the blood from the sacrifice for the sins of the people.

Inside the ark were the following three items: the Ten Commandments, both the broken set and the new set, manna, and Aaron's rod that budded. Christ himself brings to us these three concepts from those three items: the justice of the Law, the grace of manna and God's provision for us, and the authority and sovereignty of God. Everything in the tabernacle pointed to Christ.

Even the three gifts given to the baby Jesus at his birth represented aspects of God's dwelling place. He was given gold, frankincense, and myrrh. Myrrh symbolizes death since it was an aromatic incense rubbed on the dead bodies to prepare them for burial. You will remember that in Isaiah 60:6; Christ was given gold and incense but no myrrh. That's because death is no longer in his future, but at his birth it was. And death is also in the tabernacle, in the outer court at the altar of sacrifice. Frankincense is an incense and is a symbol of a priest who brings the prayers of the people to God. This symbol is found in the holy place of the tabernacle, at the altar of incense. And the last gift, gold, represents deity and is represented in the holy of holies. Though there is gold all through the tabernacle, God's presence is only in the holy of holies. So each of the three gifts is represented in the three parts of God's dwelling place.

If you will remember the way we drew back to analyze the placement of the camping positions of the twelve tribes, we will draw back and look at the placement of the furniture in the tabernacle to find a similar pattern. The placement of the furniture also makes a cross, once again giving a prophecy of the sacrifice of our Lord.

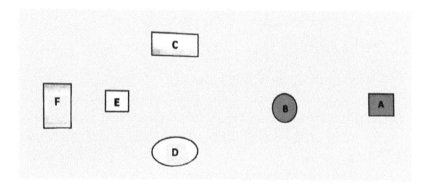

A = Altar of Sacrifice
B = Brazen Laver
C = Table of Showbread
D = Lampstand
E = Altar of Incense
F = Ark of the Covenant

Isn't God's plan stunning? It is impossible for all of these carefully specified plans and events to be coincidence. But we're not done with the tabernacle yet. Let's go a little farther.

The robes that the high priests wore were seamless garments. They were woven in such a way as to not need the sleeves, or anything, to be stitched on separately. They were woven in a continuous pattern that symbolized the continuity of the eternal God. In Leviticus 10:6, the high priest was forbidden to tear, or rend, his garment. The tearing of clothes was a common practice in the Jewish culture to express grief or outrage, and the high priest was told to never tear his robe. Since his robe was a symbol of the continuity of God, you can see how tearing it would symbolize something quite different. If the high priest tore his robe, it would end his line of the priesthood; it was a very serious offense.

Now, we shall fast-forward through time to Christ and his robe. Christ also had a seamless robe, for he is our great high priest.

> Seeing then that we have a great high priest, that is passed into the heavens, Jesus the Son of God, let us hold fast our profession. (Hebrews 4:14)

When Christ stood before Caiaphas, the high priest, Caiaphas demanded to know if Christ was the Messiah. It was against the Hebrew law to refuse to answer the high priest, and Christ obeyed God's law, though he was above it. So he answered Caiaphas and said, "Thou hast said: nevertheless I say unto you, Hereafter shall ye see the Son of man sitting on the right hand of power, and coming in the clouds of heave." Or loosely paraphrased, he said, "You said it, buddy." What happened next is interesting. Caiaphas was outraged at Christ's answer.

> Then the high priest rent his clothes saying, He hath spoken blasphemy; what further need have we of witnesses? Behold, now ye have heard his blasphemy. (Matthew 26:64–65)

When Caiaphas tore his seamless robe, the priesthood after the order of Aaron was ended. That was the last priest of this type, and now, we look to Christ for a replacement. Christ is a high priest, not after the order of Aaron but after the order of Melchizedek. Remember Melchizedek, the mysterious high priest of the Old Testament, who had no beginning and no ending. He was a priest and king, and the Jews accepted him as a priest of the one true God. This is interesting because the Jews were very hung up in genealogies, and Melchizedek didn't have one. Furthermore, the Jews never had a priest and king in the same person because the priests were from the tribe of Levi, and the kings were from the tribe of Judah. But Melchizedek was not questioned; he was of God. He is also a foreshadowing of Christ, who will hold not two, but three offices: prophet, priest and king. And also Christ is a High Priest after the order of Melchizedek and Christ has no beginning and no end.

Christ, also, had a seamless robe, one with no beginning and no end, as did all of the high priests. Christ's robe, however, was never torn. If it had been, it would've been the end of the Melchizedekian priesthood. Psalm 22:18 prophesies, "They part my garments among them, and cast lots upon my vesture." And Matthew 27:35 tells us, "And they crucified him, and parted his garments among them, and upon my vesture did they cast lots." They cast lots for his robe because the seamless robe was very valuable; they did not tear it. His priesthood is eternal. He is the High Priest, and every member of the true church composed of every believing and born-again Christian of any denomination is a priest.

> And hath made us kings and priests unto God and his Father; to him be glory and domin- ion forever and ever. (Revelation 1:6)

Praise God for his eternal blessings!

In addition to the prophetic nature of this structure and the confirmation it gives to us, how else does this particular study relate to us, specifically? Hebrews 9:11–12 says,

> But Christ being come as high priest of good things to come, by a greater and more per- fect tabernacle, not made with hands, that is to say, not of this building; Neither by the blood of goats and calves, but by his own blood he entered in once into the holy place, having obtained eter- nal redemption for us.

He's provided us an eternal redemption, praise God! He's become our high priest. And what about the greater tabernacle? Well, let's look at 1 Corinthians 6:19: "What? Know ye not that your body is the temple of the Holy Ghost which is in you, which ye have of God, and ye are not your own?" Our body is now the temple of the Holy Ghost—the temple being the permanent version of the tabernacle, which was a tent.

God dwells within us; his Shekinah glory rests on the mercy seat of our heart. His lampstand shines from our soul to those around us. We have the bread of life to share. As his priests, we can offer intercessory prayer up to him at the altar of incense within us, interceding for our loved ones and our country. All this we can do once we have gone through the outer court and accepted the sacrifice of Christ at the altar and looked humbly at our shortcomings in the brazen laver. Then through the washing of the Word, we are free to enter into this greater tabernacle not made with hands but the one within our very spirit.

CHAPTER 6

Feasts

The Jewish feasts and fasts are another area of the Scriptures well worth looking into on a deeper level. Once again, when we seek out the meaning of the various Jewish feasts and fasts and look into various historical events that occurred on these same days, we realize that the feasts are prophetic in nature and shine forth with God's divine inspiration. I'd like to first begin with the seven feasts God required Moses and the Jewish people to celebrate. We'll then look at other special days celebrated by the Jews.

The Jewish calendar consists of twelve months, each containing thirty days. This would make their year 360 days, unlike our own year which contains 365.25 days. The Jews have two calendars, both containing the same months, but each with a different beginning. Their civil calendar begins with the month of Tishri, but God came to Moses in Exodus and told him to change which month marks the New Year. The religious calendar, therefore, begins with Nisan, and that's where we'll start. The months are as follows:

Nisan (or Abib)—March–April
Zif (or Iyar)—April–May
Sivan—May–June
Tammuz—June–July
Av (or Ab)—July–August
Elul—August–September

Tishri—September–October
Bul (or Heshvan)—October–November
Chisleu (or Kisslev)—November–December
Tebeth—December–January
Sebat—January–February
Adar—February–March

The next critical distinction that must be made regarding the Jewish calendar versus our own is the very definition of a day. Our day reflects our physical lives. The day begins with a new birth, continues through the aging of the day, and concludes with the death of the day just as our physical lives progress. The Jewish day, however, mimics God's perspective of life—our spiritual life. It begins with the death of the day, proceeds to the rebirth of the day, and concludes with the aging of the day. This mimics our spiritual life beginning with our death to ourselves which leads to our spiritual rebirth and culminating in our spiritual growth. The Jewish day, therefore, begins at 6:00 p.m. and continues until 6:00 p.m. the following day. An example of this would be as follows: If my birthday were the 28th of Tishri, I would wake up on the 27th of Tishri. At 6:00 p.m., it would become the 28th of Tishri and therefore my birthday. I would then wake the next morning still on the 28th of Tishri and still my birthday. But at 6:00 p.m. that night, it would cease to be my birthday as it would then become the 29th of Tishri.

There are seven required feasts given to Moses for the Jewish people to observe. These seven feasts are called "High Sabbaths," not to be confused with the regular weekly Sabbath which begins every Friday at 6:00 p.m. and goes until Saturday at 6:00 p.m. These High Sabbaths, or mandatory Jewish feasts, can be divided into three groups.

The first three of the High Sabbaths are Passover on the evening of the 15th of Nisan, Feast of Unleavened Bread on the morning of the 15th of Nisan, and the Feast of First Fruits on the 17th of Nisan. All three of these feasts are celebrated during the Passover week. They are all spring feasts and tied to the harvest of grains.

To the Jews, these holidays relate to the exodus of the Israelites out of Egypt after four hundred years of slavery. These feasts are also, however, prophetic of the First Coming of our Lord Jesus Christ.

The fourth High Sabbath is Shavuot, which we call Pentecost, on the 6th of Sivan. This feast is sandwiched in the center of the seven mandatory feasts and it is prophetic of the church. The Jews celebrate this feast in memory of God giving the Law to Moses on Mount Sinai.

The Feast of Trumpets on the first of Tishri, the Day of Atonement on the 10th of Tishri, and the Feast of Tabernacles on the 15th of Tishri make up the last three feasts. For the Jewish people, the Feast of Trumpets is to celebrate the New Year of the civil calendar. The Feast of Atonement, or Yom Kippur, is the day the high priest went into the temple to make the sacrifice on behalf of the nation of Israel to atone for their sins. This day is the only day the high priest may enter the holy of holies in the temple to sprinkle the blood of the sacrifice on the mercy seat of the ark of the covenant. The Feast of Tabernacles is a feast to celebrate the building of the tabernacle in Moses's day thus giving God a dwelling place among the people. These three holidays are prophetic of the Second Coming of Christ.

Let's now go back and analyze each of these feasts independently. Passover and the Feast of Unleavened Bread are both on the 15th of Nisan, which is in the spring. God made a promise to the Israelites in Exodus 12 that if they killed a lamb and painted the doorposts with the blood, the angel of death would pass them by, and they would not suffer the last plague of Egypt. They were to then go into their homes and eat the lamb and prepare to leave their slavery behind and depart for the promised land in the morning. This was the first Passover supper on the beginning of the 15th of Nisan, which was evening.

In the morning, they gathered their dough before it was leavened (Exodus 12:34), carrying it on their persons, and left Egypt. The Egyptians were happy to see them go after the last plague. Though it was the next morning, it was still the 15th of Nisan because their date didn't change until six in the evening. This event of leaving Egypt and beginning their trip to the promised land is why the Jewish people commemorate the Feast of Unleavened Bread on morning of the 15th of Nisan.

There were several other important historical events that occurred on this same day at various times in history but still on the 15th of Nisan.

➤ The first was the covenant God made with Abraham in Genesis 15:13–14. This was symbolic of God calling Abraham out of the world to become separate from the nations around him. That's the same theme we find in the Feast of Unleavened Bread; God called the Israelites out of the world (Egypt) to be separate for him.

➤ Interestingly enough, on this same day, the angels came to promise that Sarah would have a son in Genesis 17:16, and God also fulfilled his promise to Abraham on this day as this is the day Isaac was born.

➤ The first Passover in Canaan was celebrated in Joshua 5:3–8, 11–12, and God renewed the covenant. The book of the Law was found by Hilkiah, the high priest, and affirmed by King Josiah in 2 Chronicles 34:2–31. This discovery and reading of the Law caused King Josiah and the Jewish people to again realize that they had become immersed in the surrounding cultures and to allow God to call them out of the world and to become a people for him.

➤ Another event occurring on this date is the dedication of the second temple in 515 BC. We see this event recorded in Ezra 6:16–19. This temple was built after the Babylonians and the Medo-Persians had occupied the nation of Israel. They had, once again, become immersed in the surrounding cultures, and it had taken them some time to rebuild the temple. This rededication of the second temple has within it the same theme: being called out and drawn back to God.

➤ The most important event that occurred on this day was Christ's burial. These first three feasts prophecy of Christ's first coming, and Christ was in the grave on this day. His crucifixion and resurrection and their relationship to the feasts will be illustrated in detail a little later on. His blood was on the doorposts, and if we'll only accept it upon ours, the angel of death will pass us over, and we can live eternally in his kingdom with him. In addition, Christ is the unleavened bread. Leaven represents sin throughout Scripture; the symbolism being that a small amount grows and puffs up with pride and taints the entire loaf. Christ was without sin and was, therefore, the unleavened bread. We can begin our journey to the promised land by carrying him with us just as the Israelites carried their unleavened bread with them so long ago. Also, Christ on the cross became our sin. But now, on this day of Passover and Unleavened Bread, the day we are to begin the journey to the promised land, sin is dead and buried. And without that, the journey cannot begin.

The last of the feasts in this grouping is called the Feast of First Fruits on the 17th of Nisan. This holiday celebrates the day that the Israelites, once they had reached the promised land, finally ate the first fruits (barley) of the land. This is when God stopped supplying the manna because they no longer required it (Joshua 5:10–12). The theme of this feast is resurrection or new life. These first fruits that the Israelites ate in the promised land symbolized their new life in line with God's will, in the new land, and out of bondage. Interestingly enough, several events occurred on the same day before and after this particular event, and they all maintain the same theme.

➤ The first one mentioned in Scripture is the ark of Noah landing on Mount Ararat in Genesis 8:4. This is a resurrection of mankind from the death brought by the flood. Noah and his family and, in fact, all animal kind could have died in the flood, but they did not. The landing of the ark symbolized the beginning of their new life or their resurrection. Is it a coincidence that it occurred on the same day, thousands of years earlier, before God created the Feast of First Fruits? Or is it a sign of God's intricate design?

➤ Another important event that occurred the same day as the crossing of the Red Sea (Exodus 14:11–14). The Israelites fled Egypt after the plagues, and God delivered them from certain death at the hands of an angry Pharaoh by parting the Red Sea and allowing them safe passage on dry land. He then, of course, drowned Pharaoh's army in the same sea. This began the Israelites new life as a free people, no longer in bondage.

➤ The resurrection theme is a foreshadowing of the resurrection of Christ, and sure enough, Christ was resurrected on the Feast of First Fruits. He was the first fruits of them that slept or the first to rise from the dead that did not die again. Lazarus and Jairus's daughter died again, but Christ defeated death.

Let's take a moment and analyze in-depth the crucifixion of our Lord and how it relates to these feasts since we have already stated that the first three High Sabbaths were prophetic of the First Coming of Christ. Most scholars place the crucifixion of Christ in AD 32 with some variation as to the date. Regardless of the year, the Bible specifies that Christ died around the Passover. The traditional view is that Christ died on Friday because Mark 15:42 says that his death occurred "the day before the Sabbath," and the Jewish Sabbath is Saturday.

However, in addition to the weekly Sabbath, the Jews have seven High Sabbaths, one of which is the Passover. In John 19:30, John says, "For that Sabbath was a high day," so Christ's death occurred the day before a *High Sabbath*. I would contend that Christ was not crucified the day before the regular weekly Saturday Sabbath but rather the day before Passover, a High Sabbath. More evidence for this view is found in Matthew 28:1 which should have been translated, "at the end of the Sabbaths," plural. This plural form implies that there are two Sabbaths this particular week—a High Sabbath and the weekly one. The Bible also states, "For as Jonah was three days and three nights in the whale's belly; so shall the Son of man be three days and three nights in the heart of the earth" (Matthew 12:40). This is a pretty specific reference, three days and three nights. I believe it is a literal time frame that would not be satisfied unless Christ died on a Thursday, the day before Passover. He would have indeed been in the grave for three days and three nights. This time frame fits the prophetic events of the feasts as well.

Paul says in 1 Corinthians 15:4 that the resurrection of Christ would be "according to the Scriptures," and the following holidays will explain why. The timing is exact, and Christ fulfilled the scriptures of the Law as well as kept the timing of the feasts that were intended to help those paying attention to recognize the Messiah.

The time line for our Lord's last days and the feasts are as follows:

Saturday night–Sunday evening. this was the 10th of Nisan in the year our Lord was crucified. Before Christ came, this day was not an official holiday, but it was a day of great significance and ritual. It was the day that the spotless lamb was to be presented to the priests in preparation for the Passover. The lamb was not killed this day, just presented and set aside for the coming sacrifice. The lamb was sanctified this day. Other historical events that happened this day as well included Joshua's miraculous crossing of the Jordan River in Joshua 3:5.

What was Christ doing on this day in AD 32 while the lambs were being presented to the priests in the temple? God was presenting his spotless Lamb to be set aside for the coming sacrifice in the form of Christ riding into Jerusalem on the donkey, fulfilling Zechariah 9:9. "Rejoice greatly, O daughter of Zion; shout, O daughter of Jerusalem: behold, thy King cometh unto thee: he is just, and having salvation; lowly, and riding upon an ass, and upon a colt, the foal of an ass." This was the first time Christ allowed his disciples to publicly declare him to be the Messiah.

He rode in on a donkey, which is the mount for a king in times of peace, and he came in peace at his first coming. A horse is a king's mount in times of war, and you'll see him coming in Revelation 19 on a horse. But this first time, he came in on an ass. Not just any ass but on the *foal* of an ass. Why is it important that it be a colt?

Because one way of symbolically usurping authority from a king is to ride his mount in public. But Christ was not usurping anyone's authority; he rode in on his own authority on a donkey that had never been ridden by anyone else before.

While he rode into Jerusalem, his disciples quoted from the Psalm 118 and "took branches of palm trees, and went forth to meet him, and cried, Hosanna: Blessed is the King of Israel that cometh in the name of the Lord" (John 12:13). The palm branches placed before him were a sign of his royal standing as well, and the scribes and Pharisees recognized the controversial statement Christ was making, and they didn't like it. Remember, before this day, Christ kept telling his follower to "see that no man know it" (Matthew 9:30; Mark 1:44, 8:26, etc.) for his hour has not yet come (John 7:6, 8). But Christ came to fulfill the Scripture, and this time, now *was* his time to be presented as King, Messiah, and spotless Lamb of God—the same day the lambs were presented to the priests.

Wednesday night–Thursday evening. This was the 14th of Nisan. This is not the Passover but rather the preparation for the Passover. It is on this day that the Jews begin to purge their homes of leaven. This is the night of the Last Supper. Christ knew he would be dead on the Passover and wanted to celebrate the Passover dinner with his disciples, so they celebrated a night early. While they are eating the Last Supper, the Jews were working diligently to remove all forms of leaven (known as chametz) from their homes. They could not possess any form of leaven during Passover. It is a cleansing process the Jews still go through, symbolizing the removal of sin. After the Last Supper, Christ went to Gethsemane, was arrested, and endured his trial throughout the night. As a representative of all sin, he was being removed from the Jewish nation by this process.

At 9:00 am, Thursday morning, and still the 14th of Nisan, Christ was hung on the cross. From 12:00 noon until 3:00 pm, the sun was dark. In the meantime, the Jews were getting ready for the slaughter of the sacrificial lambs in the temple. This was done always from 3:00 p.m.–6:00 p.m. on the day before Passover, keeping in mind that at 6:00 p.m., it becomes Passover. As the priests were killing the first lamb at 3:00 p.m., Christ, the Lamb of God, died. He was taken off the cross before 6:00 p.m. and put in the grave because the Jews did not want the dead hanging there during their High Sabbath.

> When Jesus therefore had received vinegar, he said, It is finished: and he bowed his head, and gave up the ghost. The Jews therefore, because it was the preparation, that the bodies should not remain upon the cross on the Sabbath day, (for that Sabbath day was an high day,) besought Pilate that their legs might be broken, and that they might be taken away. (John 19:30–31)

Thursday night–Friday evening. This is the 15th of Nisan, both the Passover and the Feast of Unleavened Bread. It is also two of the High Sabbaths referred to in John. The Passover encompasses three holidays, not one. This night is the first night of feasting, commemorating the night of feasting done as the angel of death passed over the doors marked with the blood of the lamb. Their meal during the yearly feast consisted of unleavened bread, wine, bitter herbs, an onion dipped in salt water, a boiled egg, and meat. The entire feast is begun with the recitation of the plagues of Egypt. In the morning, they celebrated the Feast of Unleavened Bread in commemoration of the Israelites leaving Egypt in a hurry, carrying their bread that they had no time to leaven first. During this time period, Jesus was in the tomb, the sacrifice complete, and he, the representative of our sin, in the grave. His blood was on the door posts, and sin (leaven) was buried with him.

Friday night–Saturday evening: The 16th of Nisan which "happened" to fall on the Jewish weekly Sabbath on this year. This is a day of rest for the Jewish people, and Christ "rested" in the grave.

Saturday night–Sunday evening. The 17th of Nisan and the Feast of First Fruits—the day that the Jews celebrated the harvest of the first fruits in the promised land. Christ was resurrected on this day and was the First Fruits of them that slept. He defeated death and, unlike Lazarus and others raised from the dead, Christ received his resurrection body and did not die again. This resurrection occurred in the morning of the 17th, of course. The Son rose with the rising of the sun.

When he was first discovered, you will notice he told the women not to touch him (John 20:17). This is because, at the Feast of First Fruits, the priest would take the first fruits of the harvest and present them on the altar. Christ fulfilled every jot of the Law, and when the women found him, he had not yet ascended to the altar in heaven to present himself as the first fruits of the harvest. You will notice that later in Scripture, he didn't mind the others touching him. By then, he had presented himself to God the Father as the sacrifice for our sins, once and for all, and placed his blood on the mercy seat of the ark in the tabernacle in heaven.

These three High Sabbaths told the story of Christ's First Coming, and the other four High Sabbaths were prophetic as well. The next one is on the 6th of Sivan, which is in May. The Jews call it Shavuot or the Feast of Weeks; we call it Pentecost. The Jewish people celebrate this day in commemoration of Moses receiving the Law in Exodus 19. This holiday is the end of the harvest season. The Passover begins the harvest with the harvest of barley, and the feast of Weeks completes it with the wheat harvest.

➤ Jewish tradition says that King David was born and died on this day.

➤ Enoch was born and died on this day, which will be explained in more detail later.

➤ On the very day that the Law was written on the tablets of stone, but almost two thousand years later, the Holy Spirit wrote the Law on men's hearts in Acts 2 at Pentecost. This was the birth of the church. This feast is sandwiched in the middle with three required feasts before it and three after it. It was prophetic of the church period between the First and Second Coming of our Lord. This period is also known as the gap between the sixty-ninth and seventieth week of Daniel in Daniel 9:24–27.

We see confirmation of this in many aspects of the holiday—the first being the coincidence that the church was born on Shavuot. There are many similarities to the events of Exodus 19 and Acts 2 as well. In both cases, the people were gathered together awaiting for something that God had for them. In both cases, God began with a loud voice (Exodus 19:16, Acts 2:2), and in both cases, God's presence came as fire (Exodus 19:18, Acts 2:3).

Looking a little deeper, we see some more interesting facts connecting this holiday with the church.

➢ First, every year on Shavuot, the Jews read the book of Ruth. There is no specific reason for the beginning of this tradition; some will site one reason, and others will claim a completely different reason. But even though they may not know where the tradition started, it is nonetheless one of the traditions on Shavuot or Pentecost. But I don't believe it is for no reason, for the book of Ruth is the most revealing book of prophecy regarding the church. The book of Ruth also took place during the wheat harvest. Ruth slept at the feet of Boaz on Shavuot. We'll discuss in a later chapter the prophetic nature of this book in much detail.

➢ It is also notable that this is the only High Sabbath where leaven is permitted. Leaven gives this feast a very gentile flavor and again connects it with the church. Leaven represents sin or the breaking of the Law. When we don't keep God's law, we sin. The church needs the Law to recognize our need for grace, but we are not bound by the Law. We are in the age of grace, and this is represented by the fact that leaven is allowed in the one feast that represents the church.

One connection I'd like to elaborate on is the connection between this feast and the church is regarding Enoch. Enoch, the first prophet mentioned in the Bible, lived before the flood. He was Noah's great-grandfather, and his name means "teaching." That is the role of the church today: to teach others about Christ. Also, it is in

Jude 14 that we learn of Enoch's status as a prophet, and the prophecy that is specified is significant. It is regarding the church and their returning with the Lord after the tribulation period. Furthermore, according to Jewish tradition, Enoch shares a birthday with the church—the sixth of Sivan or Pentecost. Enoch, a type of the church, was raptured before God's judgment came upon the whole world (Genesis 5:24; Hebrews 11:5). Jewish tradition says that not only was Enoch born on Pentecost but also he was raptured on Pentecost. Is this prophetic of the timing of the church's rapture? We'll have to wait and see.

Another thought-provoking fact along this same line of reasoning is this: there are only two places that the "trump of God" is mentioned in the Bible. Many trumpets sound throughout the scripture but only twice do we see the trump of God. The first place is Mount Sinai and the giving of the Ten Commandments (on Shavuot or Pentecost). The second is at the rapture. First Thessalonians 4:16 says, "For the Lord himself shall descend from heaven with a shout, with the voice of the archangel, and with the trump of God: and the dead in Christ shall rise first." At the trump of God, Moses went up the mountain and met God in the clouds. Likewise, at the trump of God, the church will rise to meet him in the clouds at the rapture.

The last three of the High Sabbaths prophecy of the Second Coming of our Lord. Let's look beneath the surface and see what they can teach us. The first one is the Feast of Trumpets or Rosh Hashanah. This is celebrated by the Jews as the civil New Year. The theme for this feast is "new beginnings," and we see this theme repeated throughout history.

> ➢ According to Jewish tradition, this is the day that Adam and Eve were created, and all of creation was complete.
> ➢ It is also the day that Noah released the third dove from the ark; the dove did not return. This dove was the one that let Noah know that the earth was dried up from the flood, and soon, they would be able to begin their new lives.

And he stayed yet other seven days; and sent forth the dove; which returned not again unto him anymore. And it came to pass in the six hundredth and first year, in the first month, the first day of the month, the waters were dried up from off the earth: and Noah removed the covering of the ark, and looked, and behold, the face of the ground was dry. (Genesis 8:12–13)

➤ Furthermore, this is the day that Joshua brought the first offering to the rebuilt altar and the day Ezra read the Law to the returned exiles to affirm the Mosaic covenant.

Each of these events in history happened on this special day, and they each proclaim a new beginning.

The next High Sabbath is the 10th of Tishri which is called the Day of Atonement or Yom Kippur. The theme for this day is the mourning and atonement for sin. This is the only day of the year when the high priest was permitted into the holy of holies in the temple. He went in to sprinkle blood on the mercy seat of the ark of the covenant to make atonement for the sins of Israel.

➤ It was on this day that Moses descended the second time from Mount Sinai with the second set of tablets (Exodus 34:29). The first set he broke in his anger at finding the Jewish people worshipping the golden calf (Exodus 32:19). The Jews had sinned and mourned, and God had forgiven them.
➤ Another historical event on the day was the Yom Kippur War of 1973. Israel was miraculously saved from annihilation when the Arabs overran their defenses.
➤ Some say it is possible that this will be the day of mourning when the Jews, at the end of the tribulation period, look upon their Messiah whom they have pierced (Zechariah 12:10–11; Hosea 5:15). This is, of course, only supposition but thought-provoking.

The last of the High Sabbaths is the Feast of Tabernacles or Sukkoth. This is a celebration commemorating the dedication of Solomon's Temple on the 15th of Tishri in 1005 BC. (2 Chronicles 5:2–3; 1 Kings 8:1–2). The theme is the coming of the presence of God.

> ➤ Many scholars believe that this is the actual birthdate of our Lord, which would make him conceived, not born, on or around Dec 25. If he was indeed born on the 15th of Tishri, it would be a fall birth in late September or early October, which would be consistent with the time of the year that the census was done. He was not born in the winter. This position has merit because John 1:14 says, "And the Word was made flesh and dwelt [tabernacled] among us." The possible future prophetic fulfillment of this holiday might be the ushering in the millennial kingdom when Christ will permanently dwell among us.

In addition to the seven High Sabbaths, the Jewish people have many other feasts and fasts that are prophetic. The first one is the 1st of Nisan. This is the religious New Year, with a theme of cleansing and new beginnings, similar to that of the 1st of Tishri, which is the civil New Year. Many events occurred on this same day beginning with the following:

> ➤ The erection and dedication of the tabernacle in the desert (Exodus 33–34).
> ➤ In addition to that, many years later, Hezekiah commanded that the temple is cleansed (2 Chronicles 29:23).
> ➤ Later still, Ezra and the exiles begin their return from Persia to Palestine (457 BC). Nehemiah followed about thirteen years later (Ezra 7:9, 25).
> ➤ The decree is given to Nehemiah to rebuild the walls of Jerusalem by Artaxerxes Longimonus (445 BC) on this same day (Nehemiah 2:1–8).

➢ It is possible that the Millennial Temple will be cleansed on this same date (Ezekiel 45:18) though we are only guessing based on the amazing consistency found in the Bible.

The next Jewish holiday is not a required holiday nor is it a feast. It is a fast or a day of mourning. Tisha B'Av is on the 17th of Tammuz through the 9th of Av, and it is a fast to mourn the destruction of Solomon's Temple by Nebuchadnezzar—the ruler of Babylon in 587 BC (Jeremiah 52:5–14). This fast has many significant historical events that occurred during this same time period over the course of many years.

➢ One major event that happened on the same day, but many years previous, is when Moses found the Israelites worshipping the golden calf when he came down off of Mount Sinai. This was the same day he broke the original Ten Commandments.

➢ Also, during the Israelites time in the wilderness, they lacked the faith to enter into the promised land while listening to the negative reports of the ten spies who were convinced the Jews could not overpower their enemy. God condemned the entire generation who were permitted to enter forty years later except Joshua and Caleb—the only two spies to give a good report (Numbers 14).

➢ The second temple also was destroyed on the same day that the first temple was destroyed but 655 years later (Daniel 19:26). The Romans destroyed the second temple in AD 70, and isn't the timing interesting? I'm beginning to see a pattern.

➢ During this same holiday in AD 71, the Romans spread salt on the ground in Jerusalem, making it impossible to grow crops for many years to come (Micah 3:12).

➢ In AD 135, Simon Bar Kochba's army was destroyed, ending the Bar Kochba's rebellion. He had claimed to be the Messiah and convinced the Jews to rebel against the Roman emperor Hadrian. The emperor then slaughtered many Jews and renamed the area Palestine after the ancient enemy of the Jewish people—the Philistines. This was intended to demoralize the people.

➤ On July 18, 1290, England expelled all of the Jews out of their land.

➤ Also, on August 12, 1492, Ferdinand and Isabella of Spain expelled all of the Jews and Muslims from their land, and Christopher Columbus, who is part Jewish, left Spain and headed for the New World.

➤ During WWII, Russia mobilizes and launches a persecution against the Jews.

➤ Finally, in 2007 on Tisha B'Av, the Jews were forced to vacate the Gaza Strip and move to Israel. Many of these Jews had lived in the Gaza Strip for their entire lives.

The mathematical odds of this many national crises occurring on the same day is 1 in 863,000 x 1 trillion or 1 in 863,000,000,000,000,000.

Persecution of the Jewish people is obviously a consistent theme for this holiday. We know that the temple will be rebuilt, and we know it will be desecrated by the coming world leader. Will it also be on this day? Time will tell.

Hanukkah is another Jewish holiday that is not a High Sabbath. It is on the 25th of Chisleu and, though it occurs around Christmas, it has nothing to do with our holiday. The theme is cleansing and rededication. This holiday is celebrating the defeat of Antiochus Epiphanes IV at the conclusion of the Maccabean Revolt in 165 BC. Judas "the hammer" Maccabees and a group of ragtag Jewish rebels defeated the Greek-Syrian General Antiochus in a three-year battle using guerrilla warfare tactics. After defeating Antiochus, the Jews found enough oil to burn in the temple for only one day while they were cleansing the temple, but the lamp miraculously burned for eight days. This is the beginning of Hanukkah. Many other events occurred on the same day, and they are also consistent with the theme of the holiday.

- ➤ The construction of the tapestries, walls, and vessels of the tabernacle of Moses were completed on this day in the year 1312 BC.
- ➤ The foundation of the second temple was laid in 520 BC.
- ➤ Finally, Jerusalem is freed from Turkish rule at the end of WWI in 1917.

The Jewish feasts are more than they appear on the surface. Like so much of the Bible, God has multiple meanings intended, and he wants us to continue to study and learn and grow closer to him. Studying the Jewish feasts helps us to recognize their prophetic nature and the way that God has used all aspects of his Word to testify of Christ. The seven High Sabbaths of the Old Testament are the primary feasts, and they point directly to Christ. We can learn from the other feasts as well, and they certainly help us to recognize that God continues to work in the lives of the Jews. However, I would like to refocus on the seven mandatory feasts, or High Sabbaths, for a moment and look at one other aspect: looking at an overview of them. Remember, the first three are a testimony of the First Coming of Christ, the middle one, Shavuot, represents the church, and the last three are prophetic of the Second Coming.

Another perspective is to look at each grouping as a time period and the people represented in that time period. Before the First Coming of our Lord, God spoke to the people through the nation of Israel. It was through Israel that people received his Word, and through the Jews that people had access to God. So the first three feasts could represent God's chosen people before the First Coming of Christ. This group is the nation of Israel.

After the First Coming of Christ, it is as if God pushed the "hold" button on the phone and began speaking to the people through the church. We now have two groups of God's chosen people: the Jews and the church. God did not hang up on the Jews, they are still his chosen people, but he has pushed the "hold" button and has given his Word to the church—the New Testament. So the group of people represented by the feast of Shavuot is the church.

The last group of people is the people after the church but before the Second Coming of Christ. God has, at this point, brought the church to be with him and has taken the Jews off of "hold" and is once again using the Jews to give his Word to the people. We see that in Revelation, God uses the two witnesses: both Jews and the 144,000, all Jews, as witnesses to the nation of Israel and the world. So God, again, is speaking through the Jews. Does this mean that all believers after the church period are only Jews? No, some are and some are not but they are all believers in the Messiah. They are not, however, members of the church, though they are born again. They can't be members of the church since the church has been raptured out before the tribulation period. This time period is the seventieth week of Daniel and is the final chapter in God's dealing with the Jewish nation. Furthermore, all of the symbols used during the tribulation are Jewish. But during this seven-year period, the Jews receive their Messiah, as do many Gentiles, and they make up a group called the tribulation saints. So the last three feasts represent the tribulation saints.

Among these seven feasts, three of them are mandatory pilgrimage feasts: Passover, Shavuot, and the Feast of Tabernacles. They are the first, the middle, and the last feasts or one feast in the first group, one in the middle, and one in the last group. These three pilgrimage feasts could be seen as a representation of God calling the people of each of these time periods to him.

He has made a way for man to be reconciled to him throughout time past and throughout time in the future. By looking beneath the surface for further understanding, we can glean much from God's Word. Let's not be satisfied with the milk. Let's dig for the meat.

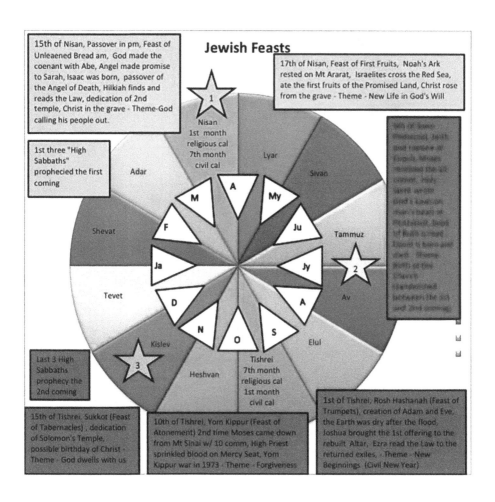

Jewish Feasts

15th of Nisan, Passover in pm, Feast of Unleaened Bread am, God made the coenant with Abe, Angel made promise to Sarah, Isaac was born, passover of the Angel of Death, Hilkiah finds and reads the Law, dedication of 2nd temple, Christ in the grave - Theme-God calling his people out.

17th of Nisan, Feast of First Fruits, Noah's Ark rested on Mt Ararat, Israelites cross the Red Sea, ate the first fruits of the Promised Land, Christ rose from the grave - Theme - New Life in God's Will

1st three "High Sabbaths" prophecied the first coming

Last 3 High Sabbaths prophecy the 2nd coming

15th of Tishrei, Sukkot (Feast of Tabernacles) , dedication of Solomon's Temple, possible birthday of Christ - Theme - God dwells with us

10th of Tishrei, Yom Kippur (Feast of Atonement) 2nd time Moses came down from Mt Sinai w/ 10 comm, High Priest sprinkled blood on Mercy Seat, Yom Kippur war in 1973 - Theme - Forgiveness

1st of Tishrei, Rosh Hashanah (Feast of Trumpets), creation of Adam and Eve, the Earth was dry after the flood, Joshua brought the 1st offering to the rebuilt Altar, Ezra read the Law to the returned exiles, - Theme - New Beginnings (Civil New Year)

Nisan 1st month religious cal 7th month civil cal

Tishrei 7th month religious cal 1st month civil cal

99

Additional Jewish Feasts – not required 'High Sabbaths' but still they show God's incredible consistency.

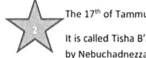 The first of Nisan is the Religious New Year with a theme of Cleansing and New Beginnings (similar to the Civil New Year). Events:

- Erection and dedication of the Tabernacle in desert
- Hezekiah commanded the temple to be cleansed
- Ezra and the exiles begin their return from Persia
- The decree is given to Nehemiah to rebuild the walls (Artexerxes Longimonus commanded it)

 The 17th of Tammuz to the 9th of Av is a period of fasting, rather than feasting.

It is called Tisha B'Av and commemorates the destruction of Solomon's Temple by Nebuchadnezzar. Theme – Mourning. Events:

- Moses found the Israelites worshipping the Golden Calf
- Israelites lacked the faith to enter the Promised Land after the spies reported
- Second temple was destroyed in 70 AD (on the exact same day, amazing)
- In 71 AD the Romans spread salt on the ground in Israel, making it impossible to grow crops
- In 135 AD, Simon Koch Bar's army was destroyed, ending the Koch Bar rebellion. The emperor then slaughtered many Jews and renamed the area Palestine.
- In 1290 AD, England expelled all of the Jews out of England.
- August 12, 1492, Ferdinand and Isabella of Spain expelled all the Jews (and Muslims) out of their land and Columbus left for the New World (he was part Jewish)
- During WWII, Russia launches a persecution against the Jews
- In 2007, the Jews were forced to leave the Gaza Strip

The 25th of Kislev (aka Chisleu) is Hanukah. The Theme is Cleansing and Rededication. Events:

- Construction of the tapestries, etc, is complete for the Tabernacle in Moses' time in 1312 BC
- Foundation of the second temple was laid in 570 BC
- Cleansing of the Temple after the Maccabean Revolt in 165 BC (this is why the holiday is celebrated)
- Jerusalem is freed from Turkish rule at the end of WWI in 1917

CHAPTER 7

Ruth

So much of our time and energy is spent on our fascination with God's creation. We have debates on creation versus evolution. We spend hours researching the different views, years spent in college, learning the theories on how life came to be. Books are written on it, movies made about it, all opinions and views are passionately debated. Certainly, there is good reason for all of this human interest. After all, it's one of God's greatest achievements, far beyond our ability to do or even understand, and it can be foundational to our worldview.

It was not, however, the only important achievement of God's that he would have us study and understand. His other major act was the act of redemption. Creation, though an enormous act from our perspective, cost God nothing. He spoke it all into existence. Redemption, on the other hand, cost him everything: the ultimate sacrifice, his only son. Creation has very little scripture devoted to it. Almost all of the Scripture is devoted to redemption. The entire book of Ruth is the story of redemption encoded. It is a literal story of a literal group of people. It is also the story of Christ and his bride in types.

The Lord has written us a fabulous romance in the book of Ruth. It's a good enough story to be used in Hollywood; however, it is so much more than a great romance story. It is also a great mystery. Ephesians 3:3–6 tells us what this mystery is all about:

> How that by revelation he made known unto me the mystery; (as I wrote afore in few words, Whereby, when ye read, ye may understand my knowledge in the mystery of Christ) Which in other ages was not made known unto the sons of men, as it is now revealed unto his holy apostles and prophets by the spirit; that the Gentiles should be fellow heirs, and of the same body, and partakers of his promise in Christ by the gospel.

This mystery is the mystery of the "church"—the body of believers that are partakers of his promise through Christ by the gospel, Christians. This mystery of the church was written afore in few words. In fact, the church is never directly mentioned in the Old Testament, and it was a difficult concept for many Hebrew Christians to understand. It was mentioned in the Old Testament primarily in types. Ruth is a prime example of this typology illustrating the future existence of the church or the bride of Christ. Salvation came to the Jews who gave the Messiah to the gentile saints who will in the end introduce him back to the Jews. It is the circle of salvation played out for us in the book of Ruth.

In the story of Ruth, Naomi is a faithful Jewish woman. She was married to a man named Elimelech and had two sons: Mahlon and Chilion. There was a famine in the land, and the family left Israel and moved to Moab—a pagan land. This was their first mistake. God wants his righteous remnant to trust him even through difficult times and times of judgment. He doesn't want them, or us, to run from those times. If you get out of the fix that God fixes to fix you, God will fix another fix to fix you. The famine in Israel was a judgment passed down by God. Naomi and Elimelech's family should've stayed in Israel and trusted in God's ability to take care of them.

The second mistake they made was this: the two sons married Moabite women, which was a violation of Jewish law. After these women married Mahlon and Chilion, the sons died as did Elimelech. One of the daughters, Orpah, went back to live with her parents. Ruth, however, followed Naomi back to Israel. In Israel, Naomi met Boaz who turned out to be her kinsman redeemer and her future husband.

The typology in this book is a perfect picture of the gentile bride of Christ known as the church. The church is an organism, not an organization. It is made up of all of the members of the body of Christ; each individual person that has accepted Christ as his personal Lord and Savior and who believes in the resurrection is a member of the body of Christ (Romans 10:9). These members are members of many separate organizations called churches (Revelation 2 and 3) that have within them believers and unbelievers. But the organism that we call the church is made up of only true believers and are the spotless virgin bride of Christ. How is the body of Christ also his bride? Well, wasn't Eve the body of Adam (bone of my bone, flesh of my flesh) but also his bride?

The typology is so perfect that it includes the meanings of their names. Naomi's name means "pleasant," and Naomi is a type of Israel being carried away from their land in the diaspora. Israel is called the "pleasant land," carrying the same meaning as Naomi's name (Psalm 106:24; Jeremiah 3:19; Daniel 8:9; Zechariah 7:14). Naomi was carried away from the land by her husband, Elimelech, whose name means "My God is king." God is the one who caused the diaspora of the Jews from the land beginning in 606 BC due to their indulgence in rebellion against God and because of their idolatry. Their idolatry was due to them marrying pagan women, just like Naomi's sons did. Mahlon's name means "unhealthy," and Chilion's name means "puny," and true to their names, they apparently were not strong men because they died while still young men and before producing children. Now, spend some time reading the book of Ruth for yourself; it really is a beautiful love story, and I will help you to tie in the symbolism within the book.

Orpah represents the Gentiles who reject the truth and return to their roots of sin and rebellion. Orpah herself returned to her childhood home after her husband died, and Naomi returned to Israel. Ruth represents the church. In our story, Ruth follows Naomi to the promised land just as the church is introduced to the Messiah by the Jews. When Ruth told Naomi that she wished to return with her, Ruth replied in Ruth chapter 1:16, "Whither thou goest, I will go, and where thou lodgest, I will lodge: thy people shall be my people, and thy God my God." This is a picture of salvation while still in the world of sin. Moab is representative of the world and sin, and here, Ruth was making a clear choice, which led to salvation. She showed her absolute devotion just as our salvation experience is an absolute devotion to the Lord. She said in verse 17, "Where thou diest, will I die, and there will I be buried: the Lord do so to me, and more also, if aught but death part thee and me." This was a life-changing decision for Ruth. She was accepting Naomi's God and changed her life to follow Naomi's God in spite of the assumption that she would probably never marry and live the rest of her life in poverty in Israel. Orpah wept tears, but her grief did not cause her life to change direction. Second Corinthians 7:10 tells us, "For godly sorrow worketh repentance to salvation not to be repented of: but the sorrow of the world worketh death."

They returned to Israel at the beginning of the barley harvest (verse 22), and this is the first of Nisan, the first month of the religious calendar. It was the law of the Israelites that they were to leave a percentage of their harvest, each harvest, for the widows and the orphans to collect. So they left about 10 percent or more in the corners of the fields. This fed the poor, but the poor had to collect it themselves (Leviticus 19:9–10, 23:22; Deuteronomy 24:19). This was called gleaning the fields from the four corners.

Ruth told Naomi that she would go glean in the field for some ears of corn and "just happens" to end up in the field of Boaz—Naomi's relative through Elimelech. Boaz's name means "in him is strength," and he is a type of Christ. You will see the consistency as we get into the story. Now, Ruth wasn't looking for a Messiah or

Savior; she wasn't looking for Boaz. She just "happened" to find his field. Likewise, the gentiles were not looking for the Messiah either.

> I am sought of them that asked not for me;
> I am found of them that sought me not: I said,
> behold me, behold me, unto a nation that was
> not called by my name. (Isaiah 65:1)

We did, however, "happen" upon our salvation. Of course, we know that none of it was happenstance, whether we searched for it or not. We know that God was working through our lives, and he was working in Ruth's as well (Isaiah 65:1).

So who introduces Ruth to Boaz? An unnamed servant. You'll remember from the chapter on the Patriarchs that the unnamed servant represents the Holy Spirit. He never seeks glory for himself but rather for Christ, thus he is represented by a servant who is never named (John 16:13–14). We, the church, are introduced or led to Christ by the Holy Spirit also.

When Boaz was kind to Ruth, she fell to the ground and said to him, "Why have I found grace in thine eyes, that thou shouldest take knowledge of me, seeing I am a stranger?" (Ruth 2:10). We too were strangers when Christ gave us grace (Romans 5:8). Remember, Ruth was a Moabite—a woman looked down upon by the Israelites and forbidden for them to marry.

Boaz was quite kind to Ruth in our story, probably because his mother was an Amorite from Jericho. Boaz was the son of Rahab, the harlot, who was in Jericho when the spies came in. It was his mother who hid the spies and then lied about their whereabouts and saved their lives (Joshua 2). Remember, she hung a red cord out of her window so that the Israelites would have mercy on her and spare her life because she had saved the lives of the two spies. So as the son of an Amorite turned believer, he probably had a different outlook on Ruth, who had already sworn her allegiance to his relative Naomi and to her God.

Verse 14 shows us an interesting shadowing of the Last Supper and Communion. They broke bread and "vinegar." The vinegar here is actually sour grapes similar to wine. So Boaz and Ruth are enjoying the bread and wine of communion together. This symbolism that we take for granted in our churches was not a tradition practiced by the Jews. After all, they didn't understand Christ's first coming; he was broken for our transgressions, and his blood was spilled for our redemption.

Naomi was thrilled with Boaz's attention toward Ruth because she understood the law of the kinsman redeemer. Naomi's husband was gone, and so were both of her sons. Ruth had never produced sons to inherit the land of their father, so there were no heirs. Therefore, the law of the kinsman redeemer applied, and Boaz was a near kinsman. This law went like this: If a woman married and her husband died before she has produced heirs for them, then the nearest kinsman has a "duty" to marry her and produce a son to inherit her dead husband's inheritance. The first son that they birthed would actually be the son of the dead husband, and future sons would be the sons of the living husband (Deuteronomy 25:5–10). The nearest kinsman did not have to do it, though he did have the duty to do it. He had to be willing, and he had to be able to financially pay any debt on the land in order to redeem the widow. We, like Ruth, need a kinsman redeemer. We need a near kinsman to redeem our soul, not our land or our name, and provide us with an inheritance. Christ is our kinsman.

There were three requirements to this law. First, he had to be a near kinsman. This means that Christ had to be a man to redeem us. He would not be a relative if he wasn't human. Hebrews 2:16–17 says,

> For verily he took not on him the nature of angels; but he took on him the seed of Abraham. Wherefore in all things it behooved him to be made like unto his brethren, that he might be a merciful and faithful high priest in things pertaining to God, to make reconciliation for the sins of the people.

He must be a man in order to be our kinsman. There is no other way for him to redeem us. Second, he had to be willing. Christ did not have his life taken from him. He gave it. He was a willing participant because he knew he had to pay the debt for our inheritance in order to redeem our souls. The wages of sin is death, so the debt we owed was death. He paid that debt for us, redeemed us, and gave us an inheritance. And he did this willingly.

> Therefore doth my Father love me, because I lay down my life, that I might take it again. No man taketh it from me, but I lay it down of myself. I have power to lay it down, and I have power to take it again. This commandment have I received of my Father. (John 10:17–18)

Third, the kinsman had to be able. If he were a man of no means, then perhaps he could not afford the expense of a possible second wife, second land, or maybe a debt on the land. He had to be able to redeem his kinsman. Christ was also able. If the wages of sin is death, and that was the debt we owed, then Christ cannot also owe the same debt, or his death would only have paid *his* debt and not ours. He had to be without sin, spotless, and without blame. He could owe no debt for his own soul, or he would have been unable to pay the debt for ours. But he was without sin and therefore able to pay for our redemption.

> And ye know that he was manifested to take away our sins; and in him is no sin. (1 John 3:5)

Boaz, however, was not the nearest kinsman and did not have the right to marry Ruth until the nearest kinsman had, had an opportunity to redeem her. So Boaz went to the nearest kinsman. His response was interesting, for he didn't say that he wasn't willing to redeem her, but rather, he said that he wasn't able to redeem her.

> And the kinsman said, I cannot redeem it for myself, lest I mar mine own inheritance. (Ruth 4:6)

He *cannot* redeem her. Well, what does Romans say in chapter 8:3–4?

> For what the law could not do, in that it was weak through the flesh, God sending his own Son in the likeness of sinful flesh, and for sin, condemned sin in the flesh; that the righteousness of the law might be fulfilled in us, who walk not after the flesh, but after the spirit.

The law could not do it but grace could. And in Ruth, the nearest kinsman was a type of the law. He could not redeem her. But Boaz, who had already offered grace to Ruth, could. The law cannot redeem us because we cannot keep it. We fall short of the standards of God, and we will never meet them; therefore, we need the grace to cover our shortcomings. Romans 3:20 says, "Therefore by the deeds of the law there shall no flesh be justified in his sight: for by the law is the knowledge of sin."

Now this nearest kinsman had to remove his shoe and give it to Boaz as a sign of his shame for not fulfilling his duty. It was an acknowledgment that he failed to walk in the Law. Our walk, however, must be with Christ. Ephesians 6:15 says that our feet must be, "Shod with the preparation of the Gospel of Peace." Man cannot be saved by perfect obedience because he cannot render it. He cannot be saved by imperfect obedience because God cannot accept it. Christ's actions and God's grace complete and fulfill the Law.

- The Law is perfect; that's why imperfect men cannot keep it.
- The Law is just; that's why it cannot show mercy to the guilty.
- The Law is holy; that's why sinners are condemned by it.
- The Law prohibits, but grace invites.
- The Law curses, but grace blesses.
- The Law shuts every mouth before God, but grace opens every mouth to praise God.

- The Law condemns even the best man; grace saves even the worst man.
- The Law says, "Pay what you owe;" grace says, "I forgive all."
- The Law says, "The wages of sin is death;" grace says, "The gift of God is eternal life."
- The Law says, "The soul that sins it shall die;" grace says, "Believe and live."
- The Law reveals sin; grace atones for sin.
- The Law was given by Moses; grace and truth came by Jesus Christ.
- The Law demands obedience; grace gives the power to obey.
- The Law puts us under bondage; grace sets us in liberty as sons of God.
- The Law says, "Do or don't;" grace says, "It is done; it is finished, paid in full."

Back to our story, following the instructions of wise Naomi, Ruth went into the threshing floor where Boaz was sleeping and she laid at his feet. When he woke, she asked him to spread the hem of his robe over her because he was a near kinsman. The hem of the garment was very symbolic because it had embroidered on it the genealogy of the man. So she was asking him to cover her with his identity. This is what Christ has done for us. He has covered us with his own identity. When God looks down upon us, he sees the blood of Christ, not our sins. We are covered by him.

> For he hath made him to be sin for us, who knew no sin; that we might be made the righteousness of God in him. (2 Corinthians 5:21)

We see another example in the Scriptures of the hem and this same symbolism. In Matthew 9:20–26 and Mark 5:25–34, we see the story of the woman with an issue of blood. This woman was a gentile and was not looking for a Jewish Messiah. We know that she was a gentile because if she had been a Jew, then she would not have been out in public while having a menstrual flow. But this was not your usual menstrual flow; this woman was ill and had this problem for an extended period of time. As a gentile, she would have known nothing about a Messiah, but she had heard of Christ healing the sick. She crawled through the crowd with the intent to touch his robe.

> For she said within herself, If I may but touch his garment, I shall be whole. (Matthew 9:21)

She had great faith that he could heal her. She touched the hem of his garment, and again, his genealogy was embroidered in the hem. It symbolized his identity. Christ was on his way to heal a Jew, and while he was on his way, a gentile, because of her faith, touched his very identity and was healed. Jesus, while on his way to minister to the Jewish people, had the church reach out to him, and we received his spiritual healing. In order to receive this, we must search for who he is, reach for, and touch the hem of his garment. In Ruth's case, she covered herself with the hem of Boaz's garment.

The entire story of Ruth is a perfect story of the mystery of the church. It takes place during the grain harvests in the spring time, and into summer, during the time period of the judges. Interestingly enough, every year during the Jewish feast called Shavout and the holiday we call Pentecost, the Jews read the book of Ruth. This is the holiday that represents the church sandwiched between the first and second coming of Christ and the day that the church was birthed. It is also the only feast that the orthodox Jews celebrate where leaven is allowed because sin can only be tolerated in the presence of grace. Of course, the Jewish people don't understand that the reason they allow leaven and the reading of the book of Ruth on this holiday is because the presence of sin symbolizes the presence of grace, and these things symbolize the church. They don't understand the mystery of the church. However, they are unclear on why they read the book of Shavout; it's simply tradition.

There are many different views from different rabbis and no consistency as to the reason this tradition started. But we know that God was showing a foreshadowing of the church in this book, and therefore, it is read on the holiday that is the birthday of the church, both before that birthday and after.

Boaz does not hesitate to take on the responsibility of Ruth. Verses 17–22 of chapter 4 provided the genealogy that connects Ruth and those before her to David. Ruth's son was Obed, and Obed had David's father, Jesse. It also explains why Jesus was born in Bethlehem because, in the beginning of the book of Ruth, we are told that Naomi was from Bethlehem, and this genealogy lets us know that so was David. Well, David was the ancestor to both Joseph and Mary, and when the census was taken in Rome at the time of the birth of Jesus, you had to return to your ancestral lands to be counted. And that's why Joseph and Mary took the long trip to Bethlehem.

There is another interesting twist to this story that I would like to address before we move on. The curse of Pharez should be discussed in relation to Ruth. As we discussed in chapter four, Judah's acts of disobedience and sin caused Tamar to birth Judah twin sons, one of which is listed in the genealogy of David here in the end of the book of Ruth. This child, you'll remember, was born out of wedlock and, therefore, was under a curse, and for ten generations, his descendants could not sit on the throne. This gave Israel their first king from the tribe of Benjamin rather than from the tribe of Judah, and remember that David was the first one in the correct line that was no longer under the curse. This curse listed in Deuteronomy 23:2 isn't exclusively for children out of wedlock, however. We need to read both verses 2 and 3:

> A bastard shall not enter into the congre-
> gation of the Lord; even to his tenth generation
> shall he not enter into the congregation of the
> Lord, An Ammonite or Moabite shall not enter
> into the congregation of the Lord; even to their

tenth generation shall they not enter into the congregation of the Lord forever.

But this appears inconsistent because Ruth and Boaz begot Obed; Obed begot Jesse, and Jesse begot David. That is not ten generations, so why is David not under the curse that would prevent him from being king? Because this is a book of grace and salvation through the mercy of God. It's about the church, and we are not bound by the law. Judah was held to the standard of God's law in Genesis. But Boaz, as a type of Christ, and Ruth, as a type of the church, are not bound to the standard because of the grace of God.

This is not to say that sin is acceptable because of the grace of God. As Paul said, shall we then sin? God forbid. Grace does not allow us to sin; it is still disgusting in the eyes of God—something he cannot and will not look upon. The standard has not changed, but rather, the penalty has been paid so that Christ will cover it with the hem of his garment, his identity; he washes it away, removes it as far as the east is from the west, and God sees it no more.

Mercy is not receiving what we deserve, and God has granted us mercy by not giving us the penalty we deserve for our sins. Grace is even more. It is getting what you don't deserve. God has granted us redemption and an eternal inheritance. Something, indeed, that I don't deserve. He who is born once will die twice. He who is born twice will die once. Without the grace, none of us would be able to see our Lord or stand in the presence and glory of God.

Indeed, the book of Ruth shines with grace and mercy and shows us a foreshadowing of the Messiah; the Jews were to look for and provide the gentiles who weren't even looking for him with a kinsman, redemption, and an eternal inheritance, paid in full!

CHAPTER 8

Prophetic Math

Math, maybe it's not your favorite subject, but you'd be surprised how often numbers play a role in the Bible. We all know that God is the ultimate artist, producing visual wonders that artists and photographers over thousands of years have attempted to imitate but have never been capable of truly producing an equal. He is also the ultimate scientist, with a grasp and understanding of how to create a perfect natural balance, the inventor of the laws of physics, and such a complicated view of how to create life and make it a success story for thousands of years. We are forever trying to only understand how it works whereas he came up with the original idea. He is also the ultimately beautiful author. He uses words as art, and people have studied the Bible for thousands of years as an amazing work of literature. He's poetic and makes use of all of the literary devices that we study to make ourselves better authors. That's not all. I love numbers, and I am excited to share how God is also the ultimate mathematician, and he also loves numbers. If we dig a little deeper into the Word of God and look beneath the surface, we find that the numbers and years in the scriptures show God's inspiration and the incredible accuracy of the Bible.

Many of the numbers in the Bible have a specific meaning. One symbolizes unity or the Godhead. Two can represent union, as in the case of marriage, or division, depending on how it is used. It is also the number of witness. The Old Testament required two witnesses to condemn a person, and we see the two witnesses in the streets of Jerusalem in the book of Revelation. Three is the number of the Trinity, representing perfection or the perfect and complete deity. Five is the number of the Pentateuch, or the five books of Moses, and represents God's goodness. Six is the number of man, evil, and incompleteness, and seven is the number of completion and resurrection; the creation of the earth was complete on day 7. Ten is the number of the Law and responsibility, seen in the Ten Commandments, etc. The numbers, though I won't go through them all here, represent a quality or ideal of God's or a part of his overall plan. The representations and symbolisms are consistent, as are all things, from Genesis to Revelation.

The focus of this chapter, however, is not on the individual numbers and their meanings but, rather, on the accuracy of the prophecies involving specific numbers or number of years. When we combine the different scriptures together, with their specific prophecies, we see the mathematical impossibility of it all fitting together into such perfection without divine inspiration. Prophecies of the Old and New Testaments are not general prophecies intended to be vague so that they are bound to be fulfilled in time. Rather, they are specific, with many details given, intended for us to see them fulfilled and thus testify of the one true God. Only God could know these details and, therefore, the accuracy of his Word testifies of his existence and the truth of his Word. Through this, we can then trust other truths expressed in his Word, much of which revolves around his love and grace.

The first bit of math that I want to introduce involves the fishing trip in the book of John chapter 21. You may remember that this is the post resurrection fishing trip. Christ had told the seven of the disciples to wait for him beside the sea of Tiberias. These seven might be called the problem children. Peter is known for being impulsive, often acting or speaking before thinking. Thomas is known as doubting Tomas, Nathanael is a wisecracker, and the sons of Zebedee, James and John, are known as the "sons of Thunder," always raising trouble. I am thankful daily that God used these seven as the example since I often fall into each of these categories.

These men were told to wait there for the Lord, but Peter got antsy and decided to go fishing. The others went with him. They fished all night and caught nothing, and in the morning, the Lord appeared to them and told them to cast the net on the other side of the boat. They didn't recognize him as the Lord, and he did not announce himself as thus, but they did it anyway. They filled the net, which did not break, to the point that they almost couldn't drag it in. Verse 11 specifies exactly how many fish were in the net, 153, and that it did not break.

This specific of a detail requires further exploration. We will start by looking at a similar story in the book of Luke and compare them. In Luke 5, we see a similar story of Christ getting involved in a fishing trip with Peter. This particular story occurs before the resurrection. Jesus tells Peter to toss out his net, and Peter tells him that he has been fishing all night to no effect. However, he will do as the Lord instructs. They catch a great multitude, but the net breaks. They then fill the ship to the point that it may sink.

The first difference that I notice in these two stories is the condition of the net. In the pre-resurrection story of Luke, the net breaks. In the post-resurrection fishing trip of John, the net does not break. Christ tells us in Matthew 4:19, "Follow me, and I will make you fishers of men." The fish we want to be catching are the souls of men. What would our net be if this is the symbolism behind the stories? Before the resurrection, the net we would cast to catch the souls of men is the Law. But man cannot keep the Law, so the net in Luke broke. After the resurrection of Jesus Christ, the net we cast to catch the souls of men is the gospel, and you will notice that the net of the fishing trip in the book of John, the post-resurrection fishing trip, did not break. The gospel, once it has us in its grip, will never break; it will never fail us.

I am not ashamed: for I know whom I have believed, and am persuaded that he is able to keep that which I have committed unto him against that day. (2 Timothy 1:12)

The next difference that I notice is that the post-resurrection fishing trip of John gives a very specific number of fish caught. The number 153 must have significance if God included it in the text, and it must be relevant to the resurrection since that is the primary difference between these two stories. A mathematician discovered something interesting about the number 153. First, it is divisible by three, so we will call it a trinity number. Then he discovered that if you apply the mathematical law of the Trinity to it, we discover something really interesting and unique. We will cube each digit and add them together. $1^3 + 5^3 + 3^3 = 1+125+27 = 153$. It is constant and unchanging when we apply the trinity to this number of the trinity. It is the only number that comes back to itself. It is unchanging and, therefore, represents Christ who is the "same yesterday, today, and forever" (Malachi 3:6; James 1:17; Hebrews 13:8).

When we look again at the 153 fish, now that we know this number represents Christ, we see that adding together all the souls caught by the net of the gospel, we get Christ. We are all members of the body of Christ (Ephesians 1:22–23; Romans 12:4; 1 Cor. 12:12) This is the same symbolism.

There's more. In the process of testing other trinity numbers, this mathematician discovered something else interesting. Though no other trinity number returns to itself like the number 153, they all (yes *all*) have another interesting trait. When we apply this same process, every number that has the trinity leads to Christ or the number 153. Example, we will start with 3. $3^3=27$, $2^3+7^3= 8+343=351$, $3^3+5^3+1^3= 27+125+1=153$. Another one is, 243: $2^3+4^3+3^3$ $= 8+64+27 = 99$, $9^3+9^3 = 729+729 = 1458$, $1^3+4^3+5^3+8^3 =$ $1+64+125+512 = 702 = 7^3+0^3+2^3 = 343+8 = 351$, $3^3+5^3+1^3$ $= 27+125+1= 153$. This will happen over and over.

Interesting watershed number: 2,000. Every number divisible by 3 becomes a number below 2,000 and eventually ending in 153. Example, 2001, $2^3+0^3+0^3+1^3 = 8+1 = 9$. This is below 2,000, and when we continue to apply the rule of the mathematical trinity, it will lead to 153. This means we only need to test numbers below 2,000 because all numbers above 2,000 lead to numbers below 2,000 anyway. How many numbers then do we need to test to prove the law? How many numbers are there below 2,000 that are divisible by 3? There are 666 numbers to be tested. This number represents the *un*holy trinity and the Antichrist. This number implies that there is an end-times application to this number 153 as well as the other symbolism. I notice 666 is one-third of 2,000.

So with this in mind, I will search the Scriptures for other places where one-third is mentioned in relation to end-times prophecy. Zechariah 13:8–9 tells us that two-thirds of all of the Jews will be killed during the tribulation period, and one-third will live. Of the one-third, all of them will be saved and cry out for Christ. One-third of all numbers end in 153 (Christ), and one-third of all of the Jews that are here during the tribulation will end up crying out for the Lord and thus bringing on his second coming (Hosea 5:15).

This is one of many examples of how God uses numbers and math for his divine glory to provide a hidden example of himself to those who are willing to look for it. This type of symbolism is woven throughout the Scriptures to constantly provide us with more meat to chew on, which in turn builds our faith.

Since Revelation 19:10 tells us that the "testimony of Jesus is the spirit of prophecy," we know that, through studying the prophecies in the Scriptures, we are learning more about our Lord. All prophecy, one way or another, testifies of Christ. This includes the prophecies of the Old Testament as well as the New. Some prophecy as to his nature, some refer to his first or second coming, some to his infinite truth and plan for his children.

The prophecies hidden within the Old Testament regarding the return of the nation of Israel are a prime example of this. They are hidden only because we have to put together multiple prophecies in order to see the entire picture. It begins in Jeremiah 25:11: "And this whole land shall be a desolation, and an astonishment; and these nations shall serve the king of Babylon seventy years." This is a judgment pronounced on the Jewish nation for serving idols. The Babylonians conquered the nation of Judah in 606 BC and thus begins our time clock.

Sixty-nine years later, in 537 BC, Cyrus releases the Jews to go back and rebuild the temple. Ezra 1:2–3 gives us the account of Cyrus sending the Jewish people back to their lands:

> Thus saith Cyrus king of Persia, The Lord God of heaven hath given me all the kingdoms of the earth; and he hath charged me to build him a house at Jerusalem, which is in Judah. Who is there among you of all his people? His God be with him, and let him go up to Jerusalem, which is in Judah, and build the house of the Lord God of Israel (he is the God) which is in Jerusalem.

Why would Cyrus, the ruling king and a pagan, release the Jews to go back to Israel to rebuild a temple to a God that Cyrus didn't even worship? Well, many scholars suppose that Ezra or more likely Daniel brought the book of Isaiah to Cyrus and read the following passage to him. Keep in mind the book of Isaiah was written long before Cyrus was alive.

> Thus saith the Lord, thy redeemer, and he that formed thee from the womb, I am the Lord that maketh all things; that stretcheth forth the heavens alone; that spreadeth abroad the earth by myself; That saith to the deep, Be dry, and I will dry up thy rivers: That saith of Cyrus, He is my shepherd, and shall perform all my pleasure: even saying to Jerusalem, Thou shalt be built; and to the temple, Thy foundation shall be laid. (Isaiah 44:24, 27–28)

Based on the passage in Ezra, it does appear that Cyrus read the passage in Isaiah. Wow, the impact that it must've made on Cyrus to find his name and duty mentioned in the Hebrew Scriptures written and prophesied hundreds of years before his time.

Though Cyrus sent the Jews back to rebuild the temple, he did not release his control over them. They did not have their own ruling king or their independence, so apparently, their judgment was not over yet, though the prophecy said they would be under rule for seventy years. So why did they go back after sixty-nine years and not seventy? Why didn't they get their own nation back? Well, let's look at some more scriptures and get a more complete picture.

First, why is it sixty-nine years and not seventy? Well, the Jewish year was 360 days, twelve months of thirty days each. So if I take 70 years and multiply it by 360 days per year to determine how many days it is, I get 25,200 days. Now, I will divide that by our number of days per year, 365.25. I get 68.99 years or 70 years. So from 606 BC to 537 BC is actually 70 biblical years.

God puts another judgment on the Jewish nation in the book of Ezekiel 4:3–6:

> Moreover take thou unto thee an iron pan, and set it for a wall of iron between thee and the city: and set thy face against it, and it shall be besieged, and thou shalt lay siege against it. This sign shall be a sign to the house of Israel. Lie thou also upon thy left side, and lay the iniquity of the house of Israel upon it: according to the number of the days that thou shalt lie upon it thou shalt bear their iniquity. For I have laid upon thee the years of their iniquity, according to the number of the days, three hundred and ninety days: so shalt thou bear the iniquity of the house of Israel. And when thou hast accomplished them, lie again on thy right side, and thou shalt bear the iniquity of the house of Judah forty days: I have appointed thee each day for a year.

So Ezekiel was told to lie on his left side for 390 days, symbolizing the 390 years of judgment God would put upon the Jewish nation because of the sins of the house of Israel (the ten northern tribes after the kingdom split); he was then told to lie on his right side for another forty days, symbolizing the forty years of judgment that must be paid for the sins of the southern kingdom: Judah. The northern kingdom, the kingdom of Israel, was a wicked kingdom involved in idolatry the entire time and with not one king a righteous king. So the judgment they accrued was significantly longer than the judgment the kingdom of Judah accrued. These judgments are added together, not served consecutively, you'll notice. So these years together add up to 430 years total.

Now, we begin the mathematical calculations. They have 430 years of judgment minus 70 years for time served, and we get another 360 years left. However, in Leviticus 26:18, we learn, "And if ye will not yet for all this hearken unto me, then I will punish you seven times more for your sins." And, indeed, the Jews did not hearken to God; they continued to rebel against him and listened to false prophets instead of accepting their time in judgment. They married pagan women and not even building the temple when Cyrus sent them back but used the materials to build homes for themselves. So God multiplied their punishment seven times.

Their remaining 360 years just turned into 2,520 years. So we will again need to convert the years into days; 2,520 years times 360 days per biblical year give us 907,200 days. We then divide this number of days into 365.25 days per calendar year, and we get 2,484 of our years that the Jewish nation must be punished. We start on a timeline from 537 BC and go forward 2,484 years, and we would land on 1947. The problem is, we counted 0 BC when doing this, and there was no 0. We skipped from 1 BC to AD 1, so we must add a year to account for that. This lands us in 1948. Well, isn't that interesting since that is the exact year that Israel became a nation for the first time since the Babylonians conquered them in 606 BC. Is it possible for this to be a coincidence? Not likely.

Even more unlikely would be for this precise math to coincidentally give us the exact year that Israel became a nation and, at the same time, for the other prophecies regarding Israel's rebirth to also happen in an equally precise manner. Isaiah 66:8 says, "Who hath heard such a thing? Who hath seen such things? Shall the earth be made to bring forth in one day? Or shall a nation be born at once? For as soon as Zion travailed, she brought forth her children." The atrocity we call the Holocaust is Zion travailing, for this was a persecution of the Jewish people beyond all previous persecutions. And it was after the Holocaust, after World War II, that Israel was reborn. And was the nation born at once like Isaiah foretold and was puzzling over? Yes, Israel was the only nation ever voted into existence. On May 15, 1948, the United Nations voted the existence of a new nation, Israel, to provide a home for the millions of dislocated Jews after World War II. There were already many Jewish people in the area. Never before, and never since, has a nation been born at once, in a moment, with a simple vote. This is a profound fulfillment of a prophetic scripture written thousands of years before it came to pass.

Another prophecy fulfilled regarding the nation of Israel is also found in Isaiah. Chapter 27 verse 6 says, "He shall cause them that come of Jacob to take root: Israel shall blossom and bud, and fill the face of the world with fruit." Sure enough, they have "taken root." Israel today has many beautiful orchards and two of its major agricultural exports are flowers and citrus fruit, both mentioned in this prophecy. It is the largest producer and supplier of citrus fruits to Europe, due to its Mediterranean climate.

Continuing with this same topic vein is the prophecy in Zephaniah 3:9, "For then will I turn to the people a pure language, that they may all call upon the name of the Lord, to serve him with one consent." In 1948, when Israel became a nation, most Jews did not speak Hebrew. There was a small minority that still spoke the "pure language," but most spoke Russian, German, French, Polish, and other languages, depending on which country they originated in. Today, however, the nation of Israel's official language is Hebrew. They have, just as God told us they would, returned to their pure language. How often has that kind of an event occurred in history? I'll leave you to figure that one out.

Zephaniah 3:10 goes on to say, "From beyond the rivers of Ethiopia my suppliants, even the daughter of my dispersed, shall bring mine offering." Why are God's suppliants and the daughter of his dispersed in Ethiopia, and have they ever returned to Israel?

Well, this does require a bit of "storytelling" back into the historical archives and the biblical history.

David's son Solomon was a wise man; you will remember that when God offered him anything he wanted, that was his request: to be given wisdom (1 Kings 3–4). Well, his wisdom was heard of far and wide, and in chapter 10 of 1 Kings, we see that the Queen of Sheba from Ethiopia had heard of Solomon's wisdom and came to see for herself whether the stories she'd heard were true. She was quite impressed with Solomon, and then according to the Bible, she went home.

But not all of their time together is recorded in the Scriptures, and according to both the *Hebrew Chronicles* and the *Ethiopian Chronicles*, the Queen of Sheba was more than impressed with Solomon. She bore him a son named Menelik, whom she left with Solomon to be raised in the temple and to learn the Jewish ways. Later, when the Queen of Sheba died, Menelik was sent for, for he was to become the first emperor of Ethiopia and needed to go home to rule his kingdom. He went home with a complete entourage with him, priests and all, and he and all of those Jewish people who went with him made up a group of people called the Falasha Jews. These Ethiopian Jews have been persecuted, murdered, and sold into slavery over the course of history. On May 25, 1991, nearly fifteen thousand Ethiopian Jews were airlifted from Ethiopia to Israel. This was after the fall of communism in the Soviet Union, and Ethiopia's government could no longer maintain control of its population through communism. In addition to those fifteen thousand people moved in one day, there were sixteen thousand more that had been airlifted in secret from 1984 until 1991. This is yet another fulfillment of prophecy directly relating to Israel's status.

Based on the overwhelming accuracy so far, I think it safe to say that further prophecies regarding the nationhood of Israel are sure to come to pass just as consistently. One of them that is important and comforting in today's political climate is found in Amos 9:15: "And I will plant them upon their land, and they shall no more be pulled up out of their land which I have given them, saith the Lord thy God." Israel's roots in her land are God-ordained and will be

God-sustained. I don't think I'd want to be in any group that's intent or willing to support the attempted destruction of Israel. God won't allow it to occur again.

> And I will make of thee a great nation, and I will bless thee and make thy name great; and thou shalt be a blessing: And I will bless them that bless thee, and curse him that curseth thee: and in thee shall all families of the earth be blessed. (Genesis 12:2–3)

Another prophetic section in the scriptures that involved a little mathematical calculation is found in Daniel chapter 9. Daniel is puzzled because he knew that the nation of Israel was to be under God's judgment for seventy years, he'd read the book of Jeremiah. But he also interpreted Nebuchadnezzar's dream and knew that there were several other empires to follow that king, who was symbolized by the head of gold, and none of them was Israel. Daniel chapter 9 is during the Medo-Persian Empire, and there appears to be no redemption for the Jewish nation anywhere on the horizon. God sends Gabriel to give an explanation.

Beginning with verse 24,

> Seventy weeks are determined upon thy people and upon thy holy city, to finish the transgression, and to make an end of sins, and to make reconciliation for iniquity, and to bring in everlasting righteousness, and to seal up the vision and prophecy, and to anoint the most Holy.

Let's just start with this little time bomb. First, the seventy weeks mentioned are determined upon *thy people, Daniel*, and upon thy holy city. Daniel's people are the Jewish people, not the church. And of course, the holy city is Jerusalem. And what is the purpose of the seventy weeks that God is referencing? To finish the transgression and make an end to sins, reconcile for iniquity, and bring in everlasting righteousness. This does not talk about Israel becoming a nation but rather is a time period in which God is dealing with the Jewish nation. The seventy weeks are better translated as the seventy sevens or seventy groups of seven years each.

When does this specific time period begin? Verse 25 tells us,

> Know therefore and understand, that from the going forth of the commandment to restore and to build Jerusalem unto the Messiah the Prince shall be seven weeks, and threescore and two weeks: the street shall be built again, and the wall even in troublous times.

Although it is true that Cyrus sent many Jews back to Jerusalem to rebuild the temple in 537 BC, that isn't when this particular clock starts. The angel Gabriel said, "From the going forth of the commandment to restore and build *Jerusalem,*" and then says, "The street shall be built again, and the wall." When was the commandment issued to rebuild the *walls* of the city? We go to Nehemiah 2:1–8 for this answer:

> And it came to pass in the month of Nisan, in the twentieth year of Artaxerxes the king, that wine was before him: and I took up the wine, and gave it unto the king. Now I had not been before-time sad in his presence. Wherefore the king said unto me, why is thy countenance sad, seeing thou art not sick? This is nothing else but sorrow of heart, then I was very sore afraid, and said unto the king, Let the king live forever: why should not my countenance be sad, when the city, the place of my fathers' sepulchers, lieth waste, and the gates thereof are consumed with fire? Then the king said unto me, for what doest thou make request? So I prayed to the God of heaven. And I said unto the king, if it please the king, and if

thy servant have found favor in thy sight, that thou wouldest send me unto Judah, unto the city of my fathers' sepulchers, that I may build it. And the king said unto me (the queen also sitting by him) For how long shall thy journey be? And when wilt thou return? So it pleased the king to send me; and I set him a time. Moreover I said unto the king, If it please the king, let letters be given me to the governors beyond the river, that they may convey me over till I come into Judah; and a letter unto Asaph the keeper of the king's forest, that he may give me timber to make beams for the gates of the palace which appertained to the house, and for the wall of the city, and for the house that I shall enter into. And the king granted me, according to the good hand of my God upon me.

So Nehemiah gets permission to go back to Jerusalem and rebuild the city and its walls. This king, known as Artaxerxes Longimonus, is the stepson of Esther. King Xerxes and Vashti were the parents of Artaxerxes Longimonus. You'll remember from the book of Esther that King Xerxes banned Queen Vashti and later marries Esther. And on March 14, 445 BC, Artaxerxes Longimonus gave Nehemiah permission to go back and rebuild the walls, and this is what started the time clock spoken of in Daniel.

More in Daniel 9:25, we see a specific division of the weeks. From the commandment to rebuild the walls "unto the Messiah the Prince shall be seven weeks and threescore and two weeks." There is a definite division here at sixty-nine weeks, and we're going to look at that closely in a moment, but the first division mentioned is the first seven weeks, which adds up to forty-nine years (seven sevens). After this time period, the city of Jerusalem was restored, so that was the event that precipitated the division in this scripture.

The Messiah, the Prince, is marked after sixty-nine weeks from March 14, 445 BC, and obviously, this is related to the coming of

Christ. Sixty-nine weeks or sixty-nine groups of seven years each is a total of 483 years. Keep in mind that these are 360-day years, so we'll multiply the 483 years times 360 days which gives us 173,880 days. Divide this by 365.25 days in our year and you get 476.057 years. The years 445–476 BC puts you at AD 31. Remember that there is no year 0; it goes from 1 BC to AD 1, then you will find yourself on April 4 of the year AD 32. Since Jesus was thirty years old at the beginning of his ministry, and he served for three years before he was crucified, if he died in AD 32 and there is no 0 BC, then his birthdate is 2 BC. The traditional date for his birth is 4 BC, but that is based on Josephus's account of an eclipse that occurred shortly before Herod's death. However, there is controversy on the date of this eclipse, and it is now known to have occurred in 1 BC, not 4 BC, which means that Herod died in 1 BC. Thus, Christ could have been born anytime before this date. According to the Magillath Ta'anith, an ancient Jewish scroll contemporary with Jesus, Herod died on January 14, 1 BC. The following historians, Tertullian (born AD 160), Irenaeus (born about AD 100), and Eusebius (AD 264–340) all give the birth of Christ as 2 BC. This makes the sixty-nine weeks of Daniel amazingly accurate.

In verse 26 of Daniel chapter 9, it specifies that "after threescore and two weeks [from when the first 7 weeks are complete, remember from the previous verse] shall Messiah be cut off, but not for himself." The rejection of the Messiah by the Jewish nation was the Messiah being cut off and not for himself. This occurred the exact day that it was prophesied, and it ended the sixty-nine-week period that God was dealing with the nation of Israel. There is still another week to come, but there is a gap represented by the rest of verse 26 when it briefly explains some other historical events that occur much later. This includes the destruction of the temple which happened in AD 70, all during the "gap" period between the sixty-ninth and seventieth week.

This gap period is the age of the church. God has put his dealings with Israel on hold because they have rejected the Messiah, but others have accepted him. Jesus weeps over Jerusalem in Luke 19: 42–44 and gives another prophecy regarding the destruction of the temple which occurs in AD 70 and left not one stone upon another and references that they knew not the time of their visitation. They had all of these scriptures in Daniel, and they should have known the dates that their Messiah would come. They were held accountable for not knowing and studying God's Word. Jesus said,

> If thou hadst known, even thou, at least in this thy day, the things which belong unto thy peace! But now they are hid from thine eyes. For the days shall come upon thee that thine enemies shall cast a trench about thee and compass thee round, and keep thee in on every side, and shall lay thee even with the ground, and thy children within thee; and they shall not leave in thee one stone upon another; because thou knewest not the time of thy visitation.

From the end of the sixty-nine weeks until the beginning of the seventieth week is the parenthetical period of the church.

Daniel chapter 9 then begins to explain, briefly, the seventieth week. Verse 27 says,

> And he shall confirm the covenant with many for one week: and in the midst of the week he shall cause the sacrifice and the oblation to cease, and for the overspreading of abominations he shall make it desolate, even until the consummation, and that determined shall be poured upon the desolate.

Daniel shows us the seven-year tribulation period in one verse—a period also known as the seventieth week of Daniel. What Daniel reveals in one verse, Matthew reveals in more detail in one chapter (Matthew 24), and Revelation reveals in even more detail in one book. At this point, the parenthetical time period of the church is over; the church is raptured at the beginning of the tribulation period, and God continues his seventy weeks of Daniel and cleanses the Jewish nation. Once again, the accuracy of the Scriptures is testimony to God's inspiration of the Bible. And since the sixty-nine weeks were fulfilled to the day, with complete accuracy, it lends credibility to the fact that the seventieth week will also be fulfilled just as God has said through his Word.

One of the purposes of God giving us these prophecies ahead of time is to show the credible nature of his Word, to testify of the truth of his Son, and to provide us with evidence of the one true God. Many people approach me and ask me how I know that the Christian God is the real one. How do you that it's not Allah or Buddha or someone else? After all, the Muslim extremist has complete faith in Allah, faith that his god is the true god, or he wouldn't blow himself up for that god. No one sacrifices their own life or the lives of their children for a belief that they think might be true. They believe it. How do I know which religion is the right religion? My answer? Prophecy.

Certainly, when I first believed, it was strictly by faith, for I knew no prophecy. But the accuracy and prophetic nature of the Bible testifies to its truth. It is not possible for all of these things to be mere coincidence nor is it possible for the book to be written by mere men. No one could've fashioned so complicated a fabric as the tapestry of the Scriptures without the inspiration of God. And certainly, no group of men separated by hundreds of years, cultures, locations, all writing alone and then putting it together into one book then has this level of consistency of facts and symbolism. Only through God's hands could this occur.

The deeper beneath the surface that I dig, the more sure of this I am.

CHAPTER 9

The Silent Years

The time period between the books of Malachi, the last book of the Old Testament, and the book of Matthew, the first book of the New Testament, is often called the "silent years." During these four hundred years, there were no prophets of God sent to deliver God's message to his people, which is why it is referred to as the silent years. Were these years truly silent? Did God really go four hundred years without a word to his people?

Although there were no active prophets during this time period, they were not silent, and God did speak to his people. It was done ahead of time and left in their scriptures for them to read, all in the form of prophecy. I'm not talking about some generic message that would apply to anybody in any time period. Through prophecy in the book of Daniel, God spoke about all of the pertinent events that will occur in that area. We read them today as history, and they are shockingly accurate, but at the time that they were written, no one but God could've predicted their outcome.

By addressing the dreams and visions seen in Daniel, we will see a testimony to God's amazing accuracy through prophecy. I'm going to combine Nebuchadnezzar's dream in Daniel 2, Daniel's vision of the four beasts in chapter 7, and his vision of the ram and he-goat in chapter 8. The dream in chapter 2 gives an overview of four kingdoms (three yet to come); Daniel's vision in chapter 7 talks about the same kingdoms but gives more detailed information, and chapter 8 provides even more specifics regarding these kingdoms. All of the details in these chapters were fulfilled later with stunning accuracy.

In Daniel chapter 2, Nebuchadnezzar had a vivid and disturbing dream. When he called the astrologers to interpret the dream, he put a little spin on the situation. He wouldn't tell them the dream because he wanted to hear the interpretation from the gods and not from men. Therefore, let the gods tell them the dream *and* the interpretation; after all, no one but a god could do such a thing. Clearly, Nebuchadnezzar was aware of the usual games that the astrologers engaged in, and he wanted the truth this time. I am certain that, at other times, he was more than willing to let them just tell him what he wanted to hear, but even he recognized that there were times when nothing less than the truth would do.

The astrologers couldn't pull it off, of course, because they didn't hear from any nonexistent gods. Only the one true God could accomplish this; an idol does not speak. Daniel, however, received his information directly from God, and since God is the one who gave Nebuchadnezzar the dream in the first place, he was more than willing to give Daniel the dream and the interpretation for the king.

The dream contained an enormous image that represented several kingdoms. It had a head of gold, which was Nebuchadnezzar and his kingdom (Daniel 2:38). Verse 39 says, "After thee shall arise another kingdom inferior to thee." And this is represented by breast and arms made of silver. Silver is stronger than gold but less valuable. God himself said that this next kingdom would be of less value than Nebuchadnezzar's kingdom. The Medo-Persian army took over the Babylonians, and it did indeed have two arms: the Medes and the Persians. These are two separate people who combined their forces to enable them to defeat the Babylonians. Today, the Medes are the Kurds in Southern Iraq; the Persians are the Iranians, and the Babylonians are the Iraqis. As you can see, the Kurds and the rest of the Iraqis are ancient enemies, which is why Sadam gassed the Kurds. *He* did not feel that he was gassing his own people. Iraq and Iran are also ancient enemies, fighting even in Daniel's time. As silver is stronger than gold so also was the Medo-Persian empire stronger than the Babylonian empire.

Daniel chapter 2 verse 39 goes on to say, "And another third kingdom of brass, which shall bear rule over all the earth." Looking back now, while Daniel had been looking forward, we see that the belly of brass in the vision is the Greek empire. Alexander the Great conquered all of the Medo-Persian Empire and then some. He believed that he had conquered the entire known world. The Greek Empire was indeed stronger than the previous empires just as brass is stronger than silver or gold.

Verse 40 or Daniel 2 gives us a fourth kingdom, telling us about the two legs of iron. "And the fourth kingdom shall be strong as iron: forasmuch as iron breaketh in pieces and subdueth all things: and as iron that breaketh all these, shall it break in pieces and bruise." It was the Roman Empire that conquered the Greeks. They ruled with force and were the strongest army ever seen up to this point in history. They also had two legs, just like in the dream. The Roman Empire had an Eastern Leg and a Western Leg, though they were but one empire.

The next earthly kingdom mentioned in the dream is the feet of iron mixed with clay with ten toes. Verses 41–43 are dedicated to this kingdom. This will be the kingdom that is set up for the tribulation period. The Roman Empire was never defeated. They simply corrupted from within, and the Roman culture has made a large impact on the culture that we live in today in the Western world. This endtimes kingdom will be part iron or part Roman. It will be mixed with clay so it will be weak.

Up until this description of the feet, each succeeding metal described and, therefore, each succeeding kingdom was stronger than the last. Each army had to defeat the army of the previous kingdom and, therefore, had to be stronger. This is not true of the prophetic kingdom still to come. Iron mixed with clay is not stronger than iron, but this kingdom did not have to overcome the last one. Rome simply crumbled away and then revived. This mimics our spiritual life beginning with our death to ourselves which leads to our spiritual rebirth culminating in our spiritual growth. Roman Empire will simply evolve from our society today. It most likely has some democracy, which creates a sort of weakness in the kingdom. The leader does not have the power to control and crush at will. Of course, the final kingdom mentioned is the millennial kingdom of Christ, and it crushes all that came before. God's kingdom will, of course, be superior to any kingdom man tries to create.

Looking at the traits and qualities of the metals given as symbols of the empires, it's apparent that each is stronger than the previous but has less value as you go. In fact, God himself points this out when comparing the two kingdoms. In Daniel 2:39, he says, "After thee shall arise another kingdom inferior to thee." If the following kingdom is stronger, why does God call it inferior? Why does God choose the metals that he chose showing them stronger but lower in value as you go?

There are two good theories for this. One theory states that each kingdom grants less power to their ruling king than the kingdom that precedes. The Babylonian king was the ultimate authority; he could do anything he wanted. The Medo-Persian king could not. He could not, for example, change a law that he had already sent out. We see that in the story of Daniel in the lion's den. In Daniel 6:15–16, we see an example of the king's limitations:

> Then these men assembled unto the king, and said unto the king, Know, O king, that the law of the Medes and Persians is, that no decree nor statute which he king establisheth may be changed. Then the king commanded, and they brought Daniel and cast him into the den of lions. Now the king spake and said unto Daniel, Thy God whom thou servest continually, he will deliver thee.

The king was saddened by how Daniel was trapped by the law the king himself created because he liked Daniel. But he could do nothing about it. So some say that the limitations of the king made the second kingdom inferior to the Babylonian kingdom. This pattern continues since the Greek Empire started the idea of a sort of democracy, and this weakened the position of the leader. Rome then had even more limitations for the leader since they had a senate that was voted in by citizens of Rome, and this senate hampered Caesar much. This is one very possible position.

The second theory strikes me more as truth, though they could both be true. It is also possible that the value of the metal is related to morality in the leaders and the culture of their society. Nebuchadnezzar was a pagan but appears to be converted by the end of his rule. He, at the very least, acknowledges God as the one true God. He is the one who wrote the entire chapter 4 of the book of Daniel, and verses 34–37 of that chapter are praises and glory given to God. Darius, the king of the Medes, acknowledges God's superiority in Daniel 6:26–27. He never calls God *his* God though. Darius always call him the God of Daniel. The Greek Empire demanded that all people learn the Greek language which facilitated the spreading of the gospel hundreds of years later. However, Alexander the Great never acknowledged the true God at all. Furthermore, the Greek society was riddled with idol worship, immorality, homosexuality, and pedophilia. We look further and look at the Roman Empire and see an even greater deterioration of morality and indulgence in the baseness of human nature in all of its ugliness. The entire empire corrupted from the inside out. Not only is it immersed in the same types of immorality as the Greeks and did not acknowledge God but also they threw Christians to the lions and sacked Jerusalem. From God's perspective, this was not a glorious culture.

The final kingdom holds the highest value. At first glance, a stone is worthless, but in the reading of the Bible, we realize it holds the greatest value of all. The rock, or stone, always symbolizes Christ. He is the rock that followed them in the wilderness (1 Corinthians 10:4); he is the rock that Moses struck the first time in Exodus 17, and the rock that Moses was supposed to speak to in Numbers 20. He is the rock that Moses hid in the cleft to see God in Exodus 33; he is the head of the cornerstone (Psalm 118:22) and the rock upon which the church was to be built (Matthew 16:18). Jesus is always the rock, which makes a simple stone the most valuable of all elements.

We now know how God interpreted the dream of Nebuchadnezzar, and we should compare this to the visions of Daniel.

In chapter 7, we see these same kingdoms represented to Daniel in a vision. Daniel 7:17 tells us that these beasts represent kings or rulers. But they are not symbolized by a beautiful statue because that's how man sees kingdoms and empires. God is showing Daniel how *he* sees them, and they are all beasts. Daniel 7:4 describes the first kingdom: Babylon. It is represented by a lion with the wings of an eagle. The wings were plucked, which would be Nebuchadnezzar's trip into insanity in Daniel 4. It then says that the lion is then made to stand upon the feet of a man, showing Nebuchadnezzar's restoration to power. The lion is the king of the jungles, absolute ruler of his pride, and the eagle is the king of the birds of prey. These are very powerful, dominant, and top-of-the-food-chain animals, and as we've already discussed, Nebuchadnezzar was the absolute authoritarian of his kingdom, as many future rulers were not.

Daniel 7:5 shows the next beast, like a bear, raised up on one side, and it had three ribs in its mouth. This bear is the Medo-Persian Empire and, just like both sides are shown in the two arms of silver of the statue in chapter 2, this bear shows the alliance between both peoples because it is "raised up itself to one side." This shows that one side is bigger or more prominent, and the Persians were the dominant people within the Medo-Persian Empire. Often, that empire is simply referred to as the Persian Empire. It is out of balance. Also, a bear is slow and lumbering, as was the Persian army. As you can see, this vision is giving more specific details regarding these empires than the dream of chapter 2 did. It also tells us that the bear, the Medo-Persian Empire, has three ribs in its mouth. These ribs represent the three peoples in Israel's past that have ruled over them. From Israel's inception, the Egyptians were the first foreigners to rule over the Jews. The next foreigners that ruled over Israel were much later when the Assyrians conquered the ten northern tribes known as the kingdom of Israel after the division of the Jewish nation. The next empire that took over the ruling of the Jewish people was Babylon when they conquered the kingdom of Judah in 606 BC. We now see a bigger and more complete picture of these two nations, and we can see how today's history shows us the accuracy of Daniel's prophecy. We're not just plugging in what we want to see because there's too much detail provided for it to be that easy.

The beast in Daniel 7:6 is like a leopard—a relatively small but swift cat. This leopard had four wings. This is the kingdom that follows the Medo-Persian Empire. Daniel never saw this empire rise, but he did a fabulous job of explaining much of what occurred during this period. Alexander the Great was a very young ruler, and he came in swift and hard just as the symbolism of the cat implies. He conquered more territory than any of the rulers before him and all before he died at the age of thirty-three. When Alexander lay on his deathbed, his generals asked him who the kingdom should go to since he had no children (even this detail is prophesied in chapter 11, and we'll get to that). Alexander's reply was, "Give it to the strong." So his four generals split the Greek Empire up into four kingdoms, represented in the vision by the four wings. The four wings are the four kingdoms, and the four heads of the leopard are the four generals. Looking back through the glasses of history, it's no problem understanding the symbolism because the events match the prophecy so perfectly. This is the last of the information that we are given in this chapter regarding this kingdom, but don't worry, they'll be back. The next vision gives us more, and it continues to be shockingly accurate.

Daniel 7:7 describes the Roman Empire and the end-times revived the Roman Empire as the fourth—a great and terrible beast. There are no similarities between this beast and any earthly animal. It was strong exceedingly, with teeth of iron. As mentioned before, the Roman army was the strongest of all armies and is represented in the statue by legs of iron and feet and toes of iron mixed with clay. We see a meshing of both kingdoms in this beast. The end of this verse refers to ten horns on the beast, and this is synonymous with the ten toes in Nebuchadnezzar's dream. This is referring to the end-times kingdom. We notice that the prophecy has now changed into a prophecy that has not yet been fulfilled just as the statue showed us a kingdom that has yet to come. Verse 8 continues with the ten horns and a little horn that came up which is the Antichrist, but this chapter is about the "silent years"—the events that occurred between

Malachi and Matthew; we won't go into the many glorious prophecies about the end-times that we find in Daniel.

Many Old Testament prophecies about Christ mesh his first coming with his second coming. Sometimes, we see a messianic prophecy where the first half of the verse has been fulfilled and the second half will be when he returns. This is the same type of situation here, and we see it many times in the Scriptures where the prophesies overlap. This particular one leads us to believe that there is a connection between the old Roman Empire and the "revived" Roman Empire, which will be ruled by the Antichrist. We see the beginnings of this empire in the European Union and other indicators that Europe desires to be one kingdom once again.

Daniel chapter 8 gives us yet another vision that Daniel had. This is during the reign of the last Babylonian king, and God is telling Daniel about what is yet to come, so it doesn't mention the Babylonian Empire. Daniel 8:3–4 says,

> Then I lifted up mine eyes, and saw, and behold there stood before the river a ram which had two horns; and the two horns were high; but one was higher than the other, and the higher came up last. I saw the ram pushing westward, and northward, and southward: so that no beasts might stand before him, neither was there any that could deliver out of his hand; but he did according to his will, and became great.

This is a great picture of the Medo-Persian Empire, and once again, we get a little more information. Just as the statue had two arms, and the bear was taller on one side than the other, we see both parts of the empire represented here. There are two horns—one to represent the Medes, the other represents the Persians. One is higher than the other, and sure enough, the Persians became more prominent and more powerful. It tells us that the higher horn came up last, and this also turned out to be true. The Medes gained power first and the first king of the Medo-Persian empire was a Mede. The general that first conquered Babylon was also a Mede. From Cyrus on, however, the rulers were all Persians. The Persians attained the bulk of their power after the Medes but ended up the most powerful of the two just as the vision indicates. The ram pushing and being great brings to mind the vision of the powerful bear in chapter 7—strong, powerful, and nothing stops it. Also, the ram pushes north, south, and west but not east. Sure enough, true to prophecy, this empire did not go east. The accuracy of the prophesies in the Scriptures testifies to the inerrancy of the Bible.

The Greek Empire appears from verse 5 and on and gives us yet more information.

> And as I was considering, behold, a he goat came from the West on the face of the whole Earth, and touched not the ground: and the goat had a notable horn between his eyes. And he came to the ram that had two horns, which I had seen standing before the river, and ran unto him in the fury of his power. And I saw him come close unto the ram, and he was moved with choler against him, and smote the ram, and brake his two horns: and there was no power in the ram to stand before him, but he cast him down to the ground, and stamped upon him: and there was none that could deliver the ram out of his hand. (Daniel 8:5–7)

This is an account of Alexander the Great—the notable horn that conquers the Persians. As shown in the vision of the leopard, this vision also shows the speed with which Alexander conquers. Here, the ram touched not the ground, indicating speed. It gives us some more information regarding Alexander in the next two verses. "Therefore the he goat waxed very great: and when he was strong, the great horn was broken; and for it came up four notable ones towards the four winds of heaven." Alexander, the great horn, was broken when he was strong, and sure enough, he died in the prime of his life at the age of thirty-three. As mentioned before, his empire was split into four separate portions by his four generals—the four notable horns. They were toward the four winds of heaven: north, south, east, and west. The northern kingdom went to Lysimachus, the western one to Cassander; Seleucus took the east and Ptolemy the south.

We read on from verses 9–14, and we're introduced to another person of import to the Jews, another man who is now in our history but, at the time of this writing, far into the future. It's a very important occurrence that happened during the "silent years" and also has an end-times application. We'll deal with one view at a time.

> And out of one of them [*one of the four horns*] came forth a little horn which waxed exceeding great, toward the South and toward the East and toward the pleasant land. And it waxed great, even to the host of heaven; and it cast down some of the host of the stars to the ground, and stamped upon them. (Daniel 8:9–10)

The pleasant land is always Israel, and the stars are often symbolic of the Jews, like in the story of Joseph and the eleven stars.

> Yea he magnified himself even to the prince of the host and by him the daily sacrifice was taken away, and the place of his sanctuary was cast don. And a host was given him against the daily sacrifice by reason of transgression, and it cast down the truth to the ground; and it practiced, and prospered. Then I heard one saint speaking and another saint said unto that certain saint which spake, how long shall be the vision concerning the daily sacrifice, and the transgression of desolation, to give both the sanctuary and the host to be trodden under foot and he said unto me, unto two thousand and three hundred days; then shall the sanctuary be cleansed. (Daniel 8:11–14)

This is an account of the atrocities committed against the Jewish temple by Antiochus IV. Epiphanies and the miracle that occurred is the reason the Jews celebrate Hanukkah today. Antiochus was a Greek ruler, one of the descendants of Seleucus, and he ruled over Syria and Israel from 175–163 BC. In 167 BC, Antiochus outlawed the Jewish religion, forbade the Jews to sacrifice, circumcise, and participate in any other Jewish religious activities. He killed many Jews, burned Jerusalem, and finally, in December, he sacrificed a pig in the Jewish temple. This sparked the Maccabean revolt led by Judas Maccabee, aka "the Hammer." The Jewish people who fought alongside Maccabee fought for three years and were finally able to take over the temple in 164 BC. Verse 14 tells us when the sanctuary would be cleansed, 2300 days, but the literal interpretation is 2,300 evenings and mornings, which refers to the evening and morning sacrifices. This would then translate to 1,150 days or just over three years. This would take us to 164 BC, and that is when the temple was cleansed, and the sacrifices were reinstituted. Once the Maccabean revolt was finally over, the Jewish priests went into the temple to cleanse it, but they only have sufficient oil for one day. God miraculously let the oil last eight days, enabling the temple's completion, and this is the miracle that is celebrated today as Hanukkah.

This is an overlapping or dual prophecy. Often in the Scripture, we see a prophecy with dual applications like laying two transparencies on top of each other and looking at one picture. This little horn that came up was Antiochus, but it is also the Antichrist. Antiochus is a foreshadowing of the Antichrist and, just as Antiochus did, the Antichrist will desecrate the temple and cause the sacrifices to cease during the tribulation period. This, of course, means there must be a temple for the Jews to be doing their sacrifices, or the Antichrist could not do what has been prophesied, and right now, there is no temple in Jerusalem. We see more of this dual prophecy in chapter 11, but again, end-times prophecies are another subject.

One purpose of these prophesies is to encourage believing Jews in the time period ahead—a time of silence. The time period between Malachi and Matthew was four hundred years—an era when there was no anointed prophet to speak to the Jewish people and a time period when the Old Testament was considered complete. God had not abandoned the Israelites though. He warned them in the book of Daniel regarding their future and many events that would occur. The events prophesied were very specific in the telling. I'm sure those reading ahead of time were left with many questions just as we are when reading prophesies yet to come. But when they are fulfilled, it all fits into place and makes perfect sense. It's not a coincidence that there was just the right number of kingdoms mentioned. It's no coincidence that Alexander the Great left his kingdom to four generals, not three or two. The exact number as the number of heads in the vision of the beast and the horns on the goat. It's mathematically impossible for this number of prophecies to come about with the type of accuracy that we see without divine inspirations.

It gets even more specific in Daniel chapter 11. Stated as prophecy in Daniel's time, it is now all recorded history. We can look back into history and actually fill in the names of the people that the prophecy was talking about and see that these very specific prophecies were fulfilled to the minutest detail.

He begins with the vision in verses 2 and 3:

> And now will I show thee the truth. Behold there shall stand up yet three kings in Persia; and the fourth shall be far richer than they all: and by his strength through his riches he shall stir up all against the realm of Grecia. And a mighty king shall stand up, that shall rule with great dominion, and do according to his will.

Daniel is writing during the reign of Darius, the Mede, during the Medo-Persian Empire. These two people co-reigned for a time, but the Medes were overshadowed by the Persians, and even today, we often just call it the Persian Empire. Remember that this empire was prophesied by Daniel earlier in his life during the Babylonian rule. The empire was represented by the arms of silver in the statue of chapter 2; the bear tipped on its side in chapter 7 and the ram of chapter 8 with one horn higher than the other. But Daniel sees that there are four kings of Persia yet to come, and the ruling one isn't one of them; for one thing, the currently ruling one is Darius, who is a Mede. After Darius, the Mede, all of the kings were Persians just as Daniel's vision showed. The first was Cyrus (550–530 BC) followed by Cambyses who ruled from 529—521 BC then followed by Darius I from 521–487 BC. Daniel states that the fourth will be far richer than them all and that he would stir up all against the realm of Grecia.

The fourth Persian king is Esther's king known as Xerxes or Ahasuerus. He was very wealthy, as seen in his exorbitant spending habits and long parties and celebrations seen in the book of Esther. History tells us how Xerxes loved to flaunt his wealth. He also engaged in a battle with the Greeks called the Battle of Thermopylae. Ultimately, after this battle with the Greeks, the Persians were forced to retreat to prevent rebellion back home in Persia, and the Persians never conquered the Greeks. However, the invasion motivated the cohesion of the Greek city states into one unified empire. This set the stage for the rise of Alexander the Great—the mighty king mentioned in verse 3 and also the belly of brass in chapter 2, the leopard of chapter 7, and the he-goat of chapter 8. You notice that every time Daniel is given another view of the empires, he is given additional information providing more and more detail.

Verse four 4 on to say,

> And when he shall stand up, his kingdom shall be broken, and shall be divided toward the four winds of heaven; and not to his posterity, nor according to his dominion which he ruled: for his kingdom shall be plucked up, even for others beside those.

Alexander the Great's kingdom was broken while he still stood because he was young and strong and in full conquer mode when he died. He was only thirty-three when he died and left his kingdom to his four generals, not to his posterity. Amazing that the Scripture is even so detailed as to tell us that Alexander the Great did not leave his kingdom to his children, or posterity, as was the custom of the day. Alexander the Great had no children, yet he was, after all, only thirty-three when he died. Regardless of the reasons, some of which are still debated by historians, the scriptural prophecy is once again proven to be true to the minutest detail. When verse 4 says that it would be divided to the four winds of heaven, this is again in reference to Alexander dividing his empire on his deathbed between his four generals. Cassander, who took over the western part of the kingdom had Europe. Lysimachus took the north including Turkey. Seleucus was in the east holding the kingdom of the Middle East with his capital in Syria, Damascus. Ptolemy took the southern kingdom in Africa with his capital in Alexanderia, Egypt. One to the north of Israel, one south, one east, and one west just as Daniel said.

The following verses tell a very interesting story:

> And the king of the south shall be strong, and one of his princes; and he shall be strong above him, and have dominion; his dominion shall be a great dominion. And in the end of years they shall join themselves together; for the king's daughter of the south shall come to the king of the north to make an agreement; but she shall not retain the power of the arm; neither shall he stand, nor his arm: but she shall be given up, and they that brought her, and he that begat her, and he that strengthened her in these times. But out of the branch of her roots shall one stand up in estate, which shall come with an army, and shall enter into the fortress of the king of the north and shall deal against them and shall prevail. Ans shall also carry captives into Egypt their gods, with their princes, and with their precious vessels of silver and of gold; and he shall continue more years than the king of the north. So the king of the south shall come into his kingdom, and shall return to his own land. (Daniel 11:5–9)

The king of the south is a descendant of the original Ptolemy that ruled from Egypt. His name was Ptolemy Philadelphus. He gave his daughter, Berenice, to the king of the north, Antiochus Theos, of the Seleucid Empire located in Syria. This was, of course, a common political move to make peace through the intermarriage of empires. Antiochus had been married to a woman named Laodice but had divorced her before taking Berenice as wife. Two years after Antiochus married Berenice, her father, king of Egypt, died. Antiochus no longer saw the need to keep her, so he put her away, with her small son, and remarried Laodice. Laodice then poisoned and killed her husband, Antiochus Theos, and ordered the murder of Berenice and her small son. Thus, Berenice did not retain the power of her arm, just like the prophecy said. He, the king of the north, also did not stand nor his arm because he was killed, and his power lost to the deception of his wife. Laodice wanted to see her own son, Seluecus Callinicus, on the throne, and she wanted no threats to this scheme. The prophecy stated that Berenice would be given up by everyone, even he that begot her, and this was played out in the above drama. Her father died, and everyone abandoned her, at least initially.

The problem with Laodice's plan was that she had not considered the remaining family of Berenice. Though her father had died, her brother had not, and he was now the ruler of the southern kingdom. The Bible says "out of the branch of her roots" when referring to her brother, and he is the prince mentioned in verse 5. So Ptolemy Euergetes came with an army and seized the fort in Syria. Ptolemy Euergetes took back to Egypt 4,000 talents of gold, 40,000 talents of silver and 2,500 idols or false gods. Even this was mentioned in the prophecy. He then returned home.

Verses 10–14 go on to describe the wars that continued between the Seleucid dynasty of the south and the Ptolemaic dynasty of the north. This fighting went on for many years, and Israel was caught in the middle. In verse 14, when it refers to "thy people," it is referring to the Jews—Daniel's people fighting back and failing. Many Jews were killed. Verse 15 goes into the story of the king of the north. He comes and takes the most fenced cities, and the king of the south cannot resist him, and neither can his chosen people, again a reference to the Jews. The following scriptures goes on to describe how powerful this man was, how he stood in the glorious land, Israel, how he received the daughter of the king of Egypt through a treaty, and he turned his face to the isles. These are the Greek islands, and the "raiser of taxes" in verse 20 turned out to be Rome. All of these things happened exactly as described. Verse 21 says, "And in his estate shall stand up a vile person to whom they shall not give the honor of the kingdom: but he shall come in peaceably, and obtain the kingdom by flatteries." This vile man was Antiochus Epiphanies who was mentioned earlier in this chapter.

The prince of the covenant that was broken in verse 22 was the high priest Onias III who was murdered in the process of Antiochus taking over the area "peaceably." Verses 23 and 24 continue to talk about how he takes over the area with deceit and peaceably. Looking back through history, we see that Antiochus offered socialism to the people, and they embraced him.

Verses 25–27 continue to refer to the fighting going on between Antiochus Epiphanies and the king of Egypt, Ptolemy VI. Verse 27 states that these two kings speak lies at one table and shall not prosper, and this happened also. After one of their great battles, they sat at a table, and together, and bargained. But in the end, Antiochus was mad that he did not achieve a clear victory and did not get Egypt. He returned with riches but was angry and took it out on Israel. In verses 29—32, we see him returning to attack Egypt, but the ships of "Chittim" come against him. This turns out to be a Roman fleet that comes to assist Ptolemy VI. So he returns and wields his power over Israel. He stops the Jewish sacrifices and puts a statue of Zeus in the temple and offers a pig up on the altar. The end of verse 32 says, "But the people that do know their God shall be strong and do exploits." This is the reference to Judas Maccabee, the Hammer, and the story of Hanukkah.

It's clear that looking through history, these verses apply directly to Antiochus Epiphanies, and all of the prophecies happened exactly as Daniel stated. However, once again, we have overlapping prophecies. Antiochus is a foreshadowing of the Antichrist, and these prophecies will also apply to him. Just as Antiochus came in peace, with deceit, wielding socialism as a method of getting into the people's good graces, so will the Antichrist. We see this because the prophecies now change and morph into end-times prophecies.

The years from the writing of the book of Malachi to the beginning of the New Testament were all written out for the Jews ahead of time in the book of Daniel. It was a warning and an encouragement all at the same time. Prophecies are a testimony to the truth and accuracy of the Scriptures. This should be encouraging because by recognizing the detail and fulfillment of certain passages, it lets us know that other passages are also true. We can have faith that the rest of the book of Daniel will happen exactly as foretold because so many parts have occurred with complete accuracy.

This testimony is written for us as well. It is important for us to know that the Bible, in its original form, is inerrant and perfect. It's important for us to understand that if God is going to write us a love letter that helps us achieve a relationship with him, he can and will protect it so that we can trust its truth. If some of it has error, then we will never know God. We could not trust any of it if we thought some of it was wrong. How would I then know which parts were wrong? Perhaps the part about forgiveness is the wrong part. Perhaps it's the story of salvation or redemption that has error? The Bible is worthless if it's not accurate. That's one reason why God put so many prophecies in the Bible for us so that we can *know* that the Bible is true. But what good does it do if we don't read the prophecies and study them? How can we recognize the times we're in, whether we're right with God or have a meaningful relationship with Christ if we spend no time studying the Word that God gave us? And the more time we spend studying it, the deeper we dig beneath the surface, the more apparent it is that the Bible is the inspired, inerrant Word of God.

CHAPTER 10

Christendom in Parables

As a Christian, you would think that we understand the kingdom of Christians, but I find, overall, that this is not the case. I think a better understanding of the church—who we are, the difference between the organization and the organism—is all very important to our ability to accurately and fully interpret and understand the Word of God. Since Christ is the Word, understanding the Word should be a primary goal of the Christian. Christ described Christendom in Matthew 13, in the kingdom parables, and John gives us a complete picture of all of Christendom in Revelation's letters to the seven churches. In both of these illustrations, Christendom is defined as any organization that calls themselves Christian, regardless of their flaws, from the birth of the church at Pentecost, until the rapture. This group includes Protestant Evangelical Christians of all denominations as well as the Catholics, Mormons, Jehovah's Witnesses, etc.

Now, some people will get their hackles up when I lump all of Christendom together and say that I am ecumenical, that I believe all churches are equally accurate in their doctrine. That's not what I'm saying. I'm saying that Christ and John give us an entire picture, good and bad, of all of Christendom, every organization that calls itself Christian, and we can learn a lot from a more in-depth study of what they had to say.

Let's begin with a parable that illustrates a principle taught in the Bible, but the parable itself is not in the Scripture. I will call it the Parable of the second-born son. How often do we see the second child favored over the first, in the Scriptures, in spite of rules and privileges spelled out in the Law for the firstborn? The firstborn was to receive the first inheritance, the double portion, the right to rule. But we see exceptions to this so often that it leads me to believe that God is using it to shadow a spiritual truth. Here are some examples: Abel (replaced by Seth) when the oldest was Cain; Isaac, whose older brother was Ishmael; Jacob, oldest brother was Esau; Pharez, whose older brother was Zared; Moses, whose older brother was Aaron; Ephraim, whose older brother was Mannaseh; and many others.

The first foreshadowing I see in this portrayal is a foreshadowing of the Messiah, the last Adam, who brings us deliverance at the hand of the second son of God or direct creation of God. God made Adam first, and thus, he is the first son of God (Luke 3:38). He is the oldest, the one with the right to the throne, the right to the inheritance, the rights of the firstborn. But through Adam came sin (Romans 5:12–21). Then God made Jesus—the second Son of God. I do not mean that God made Jesus as a second and lesser God or a different God. Jesus Christ *is* God and has always existed as has the Father. But what I do mean is that God the Father made the body of Christ by his Spirit moving on Mary. Christ, as a man, was a creation and son of God the Father. The second son, according to the Old Testament Law, does not have the rights of the firstborn. But, repeatedly, in Scripture, we see the exception made to this rule. And in the case of God's second-born son, Christ, the last Adam, through *him* comes redemption (1 Corinthians 15:21, 45—48). Christ, the second son of God, receives the eternal inheritance. And I believe that is why God has shown us so many examples through the Bible of this very situation. They are shadows to help us understand the relationship between God and Adam and Christ.

There is another scenario that I have recently realized that God was foreshadowing through his favoring of the second-born as well. During my many years of being a Christian, I have always been taught about God's ultimate goal: the redemption and saving of Israel. This teaching has left me thinking that the church (defined as the collective group of born-again believers) was kind of like an afterthought of God that he allowed because the nation of Israel rejected him at his first coming. Thus, the church is this little parenthetical interruption in God's plan to redeem his true people: the nation of Israel. Thus, it's natural for the church to study Israel and desire to be more like Israel—the people of God. We saw this problem manifested in the first churches and chastised for their legalism in Hebrews, Galatians, and other letters to the churches.

There was error in the teaching that led to error in the conclusion, and I've just recently become aware of this. I've recently realized that God's ultimate goal isn't to redeem Israel (though he will). His ultimate goal was to redeem *all of mankind through faith and grace*! The grace of God was his goal, and the grace of God is the inheritance given to his children! This means that the church received the inheritance before the nation of Israel.

Let's look back at some scriptures regarding God's view of the Jewish people (as a group, not as individuals), and the church (as a group, not as individuals).

Israel

Exodus 4:22. Israel is God's firstborn group. They are not his firstborn individual; that would be Adam. But they are his firstborn *group*. Individuals too are sons if they believe.

Isaiah 1:2. God calls the Israelites his children. Again, this is as a group. The entire nation rebelled against him even though there was always a remnant that believed and stayed faithful.

Church

Romans 8:15, 23. The church is adopted as God's sons so that we may call Abba father. Adopted children had all of the same legal rights and rules of inheritance as natural children.

Ephesians 1:5. Tells us that we are adopted as children unto Christ himself.

Romans 8:16; 1 John 3:2. We are sons of God.

Hosea 11:1. The nation of Israel called God's son again as a group.

Galatians 4:5. Those of us redeemed from the Law, the church, receive the adoption of sons.

This means that the church, the adopted group, are the second-born group of God, the second son. Ephesians 1:5–7 shows us that we are his adopted children, and we received the inheritance of grace, the redemption through his blood, and the forgiveness of sins. The poor nation of Israel is still waiting for this inheritance. They believe they must sacrifice animals for this forgiveness, and they can't do sacrifices without a temple, so they are still waiting. We, however, are happily living our unending inheritance.

As the second-born children of God, we did not deserve the inheritance of God before the nation of Israel, but God has given it to us anyway; just as so many times in the scripture, the second-born child received the inheritance. Romans 8:23 tells us that we have the firstfruits or the first inheritance that normally went to the firstborn. Romans 8:16–17 points out how, as children of God, we receive a full inheritance and will be joint-heirs with Christ.

Some people will say that Israel, the firstborn, will keep the rights of the firstborn because they will receive the right to rule. They will be the ruling nation during the millennium—the nation that is the primary nation of the entire world. But the church is the bride of Christ, and Christ will be ruling that ruling nation. We, the wife of the King, are now the queen of the nation of Israel who will be the leading nation of the world. That maintains consistency with the typology we see throughout the Bible: that the second-born son will receive the right to rule. We will be ruling and reigning with Christ during the millennium. Technically, that right should go to the firstborn, but again, the firstborn lost their right with their rebellion, stubbornness, and pride. The right then goes to the second-born.

Does this mean Israel will not get their inheritance? They absolutely *will* receive their inheritance, but it's the inheritance of grace that we are all in need of. The church received it first, though we are the second-born, and Israel will receive it second. We have no need to become more like Israel. Rather, when they receive the inheritance, they will become more like us. They too will be under grace and no longer under the law! The church is not an afterthought that God just stuck in there to take up space until Israel is ready to accept their Messiah! We are the adopted sons of God, joint-heirs with Christ, and we have already received the inheritance that God desires all men to have: the inheritance of grace!

Another commonly misunderstood difference between the church and the nation of Israel is the meaning of "living by grace" and "living under the law." These phrases are bandied around within the church, but what do they *mean*? Were the Old Testament people saved by following the Law? And now we are saved by grace and grace alone? Well, certainly, we are saved by grace and grace alone.

> For by grace are you saved through faith; and that not of yourselves; it is the gift of God: Not of works, lest any man should boast. (Ephesians 2:8–9)

So then, does it mean that the Old Testament saints were saved through the Law?

> Therefore by the deeds of the law there shall no flesh be justified in his sight: for by the law is the knowledge of sin. (Romans 3:20)

> Knowing that a man is not justified by the works of the law, but by the faith of Jesus Christ, that we might be justified by the faith of Christ, and not by the works of the law: for by the works of the law shall no flesh be justified. (Galatians 2:16)

Though these verses are both found in the New Testament, they are clear that *no flesh* shall be saved through the law. We also have the famous faith chapter in Hebrews 11 that runs through many Old

Testament believers and makes it clear that they were saved through faith. Their actions came out of faith; their faith did not come out of their actions. The Old Testament saints were saved by faith just as we are—a faith in the *coming* Messiah, the Messiah of their future. They were saved by the blood of Christ before Christ bled. They were saved on a credit card, so to speak. The debt *would* be paid in full by the death, burial, and resurrection of their Messiah.

So if the Old Testament saints were saved by faith and the New Testament church are saved by faith, then what does it mean that the Old Testament saints were "under the Law?" The Old Testament saints were under the Law for their walk, not their initial salvation experience. After they were saved, they grew closer to the Lord, became conformed to the image of Christ, by following the Law.

This rigid Law, though holy, allowed for no deviance. The Old Testament saints did not have the indwelling of the Holy Spirit, you see, and thus they needed the Law to guide them. That is what is meant by "they were under the Law."

What does that mean for us? Well, if we are under grace and *not* under the law, that means that we do *not* become conformed to the image of Christ by following the Law. It isn't our actions that causes us to grow closer to the Lord. We don't become more like him by purging our lives of sin. In fact, the closer we grow to Christ through reading his Word, spending time in his presence, and keeping our eyes on him, the more we realize that *we cannot* purge our lives of sin. God is the only one with that power, and it is God who cleans us up. We grow by grace and grace alone. Give your life over to the Lord, trust him, revel in him, cling to him in all things; focus on him, and his cleaning will be miraculous. Learn to follow the leading of the Holy Spirit, and he will direct your actions. You will realize, one day, that you have simply lost interest in the old sinful ways. You no longer desire to do this or that. *He* will finish the good work *he* began in you (Jude 1:24; 2 Timothy 1:12; Ephesians 3:20). Even our walk is by grace, praise God, because I need him for every step!

An understanding of the difference between the church and the Old Testament saints, I will call them the Jews or the nation of Israel, is important in the process of interpreting the Bible. They are not the same group, and they do not have the same destiny. I'm not saying one is better and one is worse; simply, they are two different groups. We are not grafted into the vine of Israel; we are the wild branch grafted into the root of Christ. The nation of Israel is the original branch that will be regrafted into the root of Christ also (Romans 11:11–31). The two separate branches will produce different fruit, even. Just like a lemon tree that has a lime branch grafted into it now produces two different fruits. This is good! God has it all covered. He has a big plan, and it requires us all. Let's look at the two groups.

The first place the word *church* is mentioned is in Matthew 16:18. Jesus tells Peter that upon the rock, he *will* build his church. First Corinthians tells us that the rock is Christ, and the word *will* tells us that there was no church yet when Christ made this statement. The word *church* never appears in the Old Testament; it never appears in Mark, Luke, or John. There was no church until the day of Pentecost in Acts. This was the birth of the church, and from this, we can conclude that the Old Testament saints were not members of the church. It is a strictly New Testament phenomenon.

The nation of Israel are God's chosen people, chosen as a nation (not the individuals chosen but the group is chosen.) They were never given the Great Commission and, in fact, were told to *not* intermingle with the surrounding people. They were told to be a light to the gentile nations right where they were (Isaiah 42, 49). This is because they were never given the indwelling of the Holy Spirit, only the infilling.

1. They are the *wife of God the Father*, whom he divorces because she prostituted herself out to other gods (Jeremiah 3).
2. In other places in the Scripture, God calls Israel his child, his *natural child* (Exodus 4:22; Isaiah 1:2; Hebrews 11:1).
3. The fruit that grows in Israel, the *fig tree, the olive tree, and the grape vine*, often symbolizes the nation of Israel (Matthew 24:32; Psalm 52:8; Revelation 11:4; Isaiah 5:1–2).

4. It is also called the *natural branch* which was cut off and will be grafted back into the tree, which is Christ (Romans 11:13–24).
5. Israel is an *organization* within which are believers and unbelievers both.
6. Israel is saved by faith (justified) but *sanctified by following the law* (Galatians 2:16). The sanctification process has nothing to do with being saved. It is the growth process, the way that they grow in their relationship with God.

The church, *in its truest definition*, is made up of every person who has accepted Christ as their Lord and Savior and believes in his resurrection (Romans 10:9). The church is also a chosen group but with a different calling and a different destiny. We *are* given the Great Commission and are not to separate ourselves completely from the pagan world around us. No individual is chosen to be in the group, but the group is chosen to evangelize.

1. The church is *the virgin bride of Christ*, presented as a spotless virgin, which means that we never commit spiritual adultery against God, which would be idolatry (Ephesians 5:25–27; Revelation 19:7; 2 Corinthians 11:2).
2. We are the *adopted child of God* and thus his second child (Romans 8:15–23; Ephesians 1:5; 1 John 3:2; Galatians 4:5).
3. The *grains* are the symbol of the church (Acts 2, the birth of the church, was during the grain harvest, Ruth [all about the church] is during the grain harvest, the parables of wheat in Matthew are all about the church).
4. It is also called the *wild branch* which was grafted into the tree of Christ when the natural branch was cut off. But the natural branch will again be grafted in, and Christ, the tree, will then have *two separate branches* that bear *two different fruits*. We are *not* grafted into Israel. We are all grafted into Christ (Romans 11:13–24; John 15:1).

5. The church is an *organism*, not an organization. Christ is the head, and we are the body (1 Corinthians 12:27).
6. The church is saved by faith, but our *sanctification is also through grace and faith, not* through the law (Romans 8:2; Galatians 5:22–23, 3:1–3). The sanctification process has nothing to do with being saved. It is the growth process, the way that we grow in our relationship with Christ.

This definition is what the *true* church is, the spiritual church. The organized church is a building filled with wheat and tares or believers and unbelievers. The church, the organization, is what Christ is talking about in the parables in Matthew 13. The organization is what we might call Christendom or the functioning of the physical church (anything that calls itself Christian, no matter how flawed the organization) on earth from Pentecost until the rapture. The organization, the church, is the church that we will be looking at in Revelation. John wrote letters to seven churches, meaning the seven organizations, filled with people from various walks of life, different personalities, and different belief systems, some saved, some not. These teachings encompass all of Christendom, and a lot can be gained from a little introspection incorporating these teachings. After all, we are part of this group.

Jesus, in the gospels, begins by preaching to the Jews and trying to get them to understand that if they will accept him as the Messiah, then he will set up the kingdom because the King is here. He is preaching the gospel of the kingdom, and he's speaking primarily to the Jews, and that's a very important thing to understand when reading the gospels; it is an extension of the Old Testament until Christ is rejected. The birth of the church doesn't begin until Acts. But because the nation of Israel doesn't embrace Christ and his message, God puts the nation of Israel on hold, and he sets up his kingdom on earth within the church.

In Matthew 12, it begins with the Pharisees (a representation of the nation of Israel) criticizing Christ for working on the Sabbath. Christ *is* the Sabbath. Jesus moves on to the teaching of the house divided with itself cannot stand and chastising them for blaspheming the Holy Ghost or their hard-hearted rejection of the Messiah. He discusses the good fruit and the bad fruit, but remember, the fruit analogies represent Israel and the Jews as a nation, so this is directed at the Pharisees that had just come across with their self-righteous attitude of condemnation of the Messiah they are supposedly looking for. Then he talks about the sign of Jonah. He points out how many Jews are following him only for the signs and wonders, and that they are an evil and adulterous generation. This is why we don't have the signs and wonders today that they did in Christ's time because Jesus wants us to follow him, not his signs and wonders. He wants us to worship the gift giver, not the gifts. He informs these Jewish sign-seekers that someday, the only sign given will be his resurrection. His resurrection should be all the sign we need to believe.

Now that he is done chastising them, he begins to speak in parables about where the kingdom will go, due to the fact that the Jewish nation will not accept him as Messiah. After his resurrection, there will be the kingdom of heaven, which is the reign of the church on earth. The kingdom of heaven is not interchangeable with the kingdom of God that is mentioned in other gospels. The kingdom of God is everything that God rules, which is everything. Within that kingdom is a subset called the kingdom of heaven. The kingdom of heaven is God's kingdom as it's represented on earth. Only in Matthew do we see the phrase the kingdom of heaven, and he begins here in chapter 13 because he needs to show us how his kingdom will be represented on earth since the Jewish Nation will not yet be that kingdom. He speaks in parables because he doesn't want the Pharisees, who had just expressed their rejection of him, to understand. We know that he is referring to the church for two reasons: one, the church follows the resurrection, and two, the parables begin with grain parables, and the grains represent the church.

The first parable is the parable of the sower in Matthew 13:1–17. It is also in Luke and the phrase the kingdom of heaven of Matthew 13 is called the kingdom of God in Luke. This leads some people to assume the terms are synonymous and interchangeable, but actually, the kingdom of heaven is a subset of the kingdom of God. All of the parables labeled the kingdom of heaven are referencing the church, not all parables labeled the kingdom of God are. All kingdom of heaven stories are also kingdom of God, but not all kingdom of God stories are also the kingdom of heaven.

In the parable of the sower, the sower goes out and spreads seed. Some of the seed go by the wayside and the birds eat it. Some of it land in stony places with very little soil, and it starts to spring up, but the sun withers it, and it dies. Some seed fall among the thorns, and the thorns choke it out. The rest fell into good, rich soil, and it grew and brought forth fruit, some a hundredfold, some sixtyfold, and some thirtyfold. Now, the beauty of this parable is that Christ himself interprets the meaning and, in the process, he gives us the code by which we can interpret all of the parables after this!

The seed is clearly the Word of God. Christ lets us know that the birds that snatch away the first seeds is the wicked one. For some people, Satan and his minions steal away the Word of God away from our unprepared hearts before it can take root.

The second group of seeds that lands upon the stony places tries to take root. This is a stony heart, and the seed struggles. The minute the person endures trials or tribulation due to the Word of God they have listened to, they lose their convictions and abandon God. The tiny juvenile plant shrivels up and dies.

Then comes the seeds that land in the thorns. The thorns are the cares of the world—the culture around you, the sin you have always been embroiled in, the manner in which the person has grown to see things. His inability to see the truth in the midst of this messy world causes the seed to die.

The only situation where the seed takes root and grows into a healthy plant is but the last scenario. In this situation, we see the seed lands on the good, healthy soil. This heart has been prepared, through God and the free will of the man himself, to accept and receive the Word of truth. In this scenario, all of the seeds bore fruit, though some produced much, and others produced little. But *all* of the seeds that were sown by the sower into the healthy soil produced fruit. The fruit of the grain plant is more grain! So they are all becoming sowers!

Jesus concludes the parable with, "Who has ears to hear, let him hear." Not anyone who has ears but anyone who has ears to hear! Are you willing to listen to him and hear what he's saying? That's why he is speaking in parables now so that those who didn't really want to hear what he has to say will not hear and understand. He covers this in the next section of scripture. After Christ gives this first parable, the disciples asked him why he was speaking in parables all of a sudden. He informs them that he doesn't want the scribes and Pharisees to hear and understand, so he's speaking in kind of a code.

What did the scribes and Pharisees do that caused him to not want them to truly understand? They had attributed to Christ the works of the devil. They are the spiritual leaders of Israel and the primary representatives of Israel. If, back then, you wondered what the position of the Israelites was, you would consult the scribes and the Pharisees, not the average peon on the street corner. Just like today, if we wanted to know what the United States' position is on some major issue, like supporting Israel, we would see what the president says about it or what congress has to say on the issue. They represent my nation, and the Pharisees were the representation of the nation of Israel. When they rejected Christ again and went so far as to attribute to Christ the works of Satan, they (as a nation, not as individuals) had committed the unpardonable sin. Rejection of the Messiah clearly until the moment of our death is the only sin that is unpardonable. Christ is now hinting at this same concept but attributing it to the nation rather than the individual. The nation of Israel will reject Christ, and because of this, he will begin to speak in ways that they are not listening to, and he will begin to tell *grain* parables, showing that he will take the message to the gentile church.

If the parables are a code, they need a key to unscramble, and Christ gives us this key in his explanation of this first parable in verses 18–23. The seed is the Word; the soil is the heart, and the birds are the emissaries of Satan. These symbols will stay consistent through all of the parables; you can't suddenly decide that the birds are Christians because that isn't consistent. We also see, in this parable, the concept that the three ways that sin enters into society and people are the (1) devil, (2) flesh, and (3) the world. These three are the three ways that sin enters. The devil and his minions will certainly bring the temptation of sin before you, and Christ illustrates that as the birds. The flesh is our desire to have our way and to follow our wicked heart and human nation. We see this one as the stony heart. In verse 21, Christ said, "Yet does he not have root in *himself*." Our stony heart will prevent the Word of God from taking root. Last is the world, and in this parable, we see them as the thorns choking out the word.

The world, the flesh, and the devil are an important concept to understand the full nature of sin. We see the same thing today. The world is often our governmental system. The sin of abortion entered our nation as an approved procedure by the wicked world—the laws of the land. The devil is still active but don't blame him for everything because someday, during the millennium, he will be locked up, and sin will still become a major problem. During the millennium, the devil will be locked up, so sin won't enter through him. The government will be Christ and his church, so sin won't enter through the laws of the land. Nothing will be left but the flesh, and still, we will have so much sin that, at the end of the one thousand years, when Satan is released from the pit, he will find an army among mankind to march against Christ and Jerusalem! (Revelation 20). We will have no excuses left for our sin!

In the next parable, we will be sure to maintain consistency in interpretation. The parable of the wheat and tares is, again, about the church. The kingdom of heaven is God's representation of his kingdom on earth, which can be the nation of Israel in the Old Testament time or it can be the church after the resurrection. Since Christ has shifted his focus from teaching the Jews, he is right now, again, talking about the church that is to come. It doesn't exist when he's speaking; the church isn't born until Pentecost. But it will exist, and he's preparing them for that in all of these parables.

This parable is the parable of the wheat and the tares (Matthew 13:24–30). The farmer comes along and spreads the seeds for his crop. Along comes the enemy and spreads the seeds for weeds. Now, in consistently using the key Christ provided when he interpreted the first parable, we know that the seeds represent the Word of God. The farmer who spreads the seed is Christ, and the enemy is, naturally, the devil. If the seed is the Word of God, then the weed seed is the seed of false doctrine. It looks similar when it's small, but it grows quickly, spreads fast, and permeates completely. And it's destructive. So here, we have the church with good seed and false doctrine intermingled. The servants want to know if they should go weed the field, but the farmer tells them no. Just wait until it's time for the harvest and separate them at that time. The reason for this is because, in pulling the weeds, you may damage the good plants. Sometimes, we find ourselves in a church with a lot of false doctrine. The impulse for me and my husband is that we really want to correct it. We want to pull the weeds! If there's just a few, sometimes this is successful, but if there are a lot of weeds, you may damage the young and growing Christian that's trying to mature alongside the messy doctrine. Sometimes, we just need to walk away and wait for the harvest and let the Lord sort it out! The harvest of the church is *not* done by us! It's done by God, and it won't be done until the crop is done, and God is ready to rapture us out!

The parable of the mustard seed (Matthew 13:31–32) is often misunderstood simply because people don't understand the importance of maintaining consistency in interpreting the parables and, in fact, all of the Scriptures. When symbols are used, they are always consistent in their meaning. In the parable of the mustard seed, we see a mustard seed which is a very small seed that is intended to grow a mustard plant. Mustard plants are fairly low plants and never intended to be trees. Again, the seed is the Word of God, and the kingdom of heaven is God's representation of his kingdom on earth, aka the church. When the man planted this tiniest of seeds that has great importance, the seed grew into a huge tree. In the branches of the tree, we see the birds lodging there. This sounds nice. It sounds like a great big church with many wonderful congregants. But wait… In the first parable, Christ tells us that the birds are the emissaries of the devil, and if we are consistent, we must understand that these birds aren't good, but rather, they are the presence and influence of the devil. And the mustard seed wasn't intended to be the big, happy home of the devil's minions. This church grew into a monster that included these loud, influential "birds."

The parable of the leaven is another parable showing, again, that the church will not be a perfect organism. After this short parable, we see Christ again explain to his disciples his interpretation of one of the parables, but first, we will discuss this parable of leaven. Three measures of meal is the fellowship offering, and here, we have the woman creating a fellowship offering. But in it, there is leaven. Leaven always represents sin or false doctrine, and we can see why. A very small amount permeates the entire bread. Within God's church—his representation of his kingdom as it is on earth—there will be sin and false doctrine.

Christ now goes into the house to speak to only his disciples, and he explains the parable of the wheat and the tares. You can see that Christ is the farmer spreading the Word, not me. He uses us to do it, but we are only the tool. *He* is the farmer. He makes it clear that it is not the Christian who harvests, and the harvest isn't today. It's the end of the age, the end-times. I have heard many preachers say that we need to get busy with the harvest. This is incorrect! We are not angels, and we do not harvest! We are the tools used to plant the seeds and water, but it is God who brings in the harvest.

The next two parables are similar. In one, the man finds a treasure in a field. He sells all that he has so that that he can purchase the field. In the following parable, about the pearl of great price, when the merchant finds a valuable pearl, he sells all that he has to purchase it. The amazing thing about these two parables is that *you* are the great treasure found in the field! *You* are the pearl that has great value! The treasure and the pearl are not Christ, and you and I could never sell enough to purchase him. But he gave everything to purchase us! The God of the universe, the creator of it all, the *Almighty* God gave up his habitation, his glorious home, to humble himself as a mere man. He lived a humble life as a child, a teen, and a young carpenter and learning at the knee of simple people. Then he allowed himself to be lied about, ridiculed, spat on, mocked, and unjustly accused. If that wasn't enough, he was tried in a kangaroo court; he allowed himself to be beaten terribly, hung on a cross like a common criminal, and even rejected by God the Father! All so that he could purchase a pearl! An item of adornment that came from an unclean animal that the Jewish people were forbidden to wear! A pearl, you and me, that he found valuable. A beautiful item that began as a piece of sand, sand that annoyed and irritated the oyster, so the oyster excreted material to surround the piece of sand so that it wouldn't irritate him so bad. As time went on, the process continued until the pearl was beautiful in the eyes of the merchant. Christ is our merchant and, shocking though it may seem, *we* are the treasure and the pearl that he gave everything for! Thank you, Jesus!

The seventh and last of these parables is the parable of the net. The kingdom of heaven is like a net that is cast out and catches all types of fish. When it's pulled to shore, it must be gone through to separate the trash fish from the keepers! Again, this is about the church and, ultimately the harvest of the church. The kingdom of heaven, the representation of God's kingdom on earth, will have saved and unsaved within its organizations. This is similar to the earlier parable of the wheat and the tares. The net that's cast, which is the gospel intended to catch the souls of men, catches all sorts. Some want to attend the organization because it makes their parents happy. Some do it because they always have. Some attend because it gives them status or credibility in the community. Some go because they want to be a part of a great organization that helps the needy. Some do it out of habit or because they found a church that makes them feel righteous or good about themselves. And of course, some go because they are born-again believers who want and need to be around other born-again believers for learning, edification, ministry, and service. There are many reasons why people attend church, and they aren't all for the right reasons.

When the season is right for the harvesting of the souls of the churches, the Lord will sort out who will be in which category! He knows the hearts of the people within the congregations, and he knows who is saved and who isn't. I don't have access to this infor- mation because I can't see the hearts, but God knows! And when it's time, he will sit and separate us out. The true believers will spend eternity with the Lord, and the rest won't. It's that simple!

Through these seven parables, Christ has given us a beginning view of Christendom throughout the ages in its good and bad sides! We learn the value of every man, woman, and child who accepts the Lord through the parables of the treasure in the field and the pearl. The Lord gives it all for us! We learn that not everyone given the seed will become a Christian, and in fact, there are more reasons they don't than there are reasons they do. This is made clear in the parable of the sower. Through the parable of the leaven, we are warned that sin and false doctrine will permeate our churches completely if we don't watch for it. And we learn that not everyone in the churches is saved not only in the parable of the net but also in the parable of the wheat and the tares. Many in the churches are not saved, but we are also warned that it is not our place or our job to be trying to remove those that are not saved! Let the Lord and his angels take care of the harvest, or we will harm the wheat.

Although this gives us a very good initial perspective of the church that didn't yet exist in Christ's time, we have an even more thorough view of Christendom over time through the letters to the seven churches of Revelation. In our next chapter, we will delve into God's view of the churches as they progressed over time. Did God abhor the Catholic Church during the Roman Catholic Empire? Did he consider the first church that began in Jerusalem at Acts 2 to be the best ideal church to model? Did God think that the Reformation Movement created an improvement in the condition of Christianity, spiritually? We will go into this in some depth in the next chapter about Christendom.

CHAPTER 11

Christendom in Revelation

In our study of the true meaning of the church, we cannot neglect to delve into the book of Revelation. In the first few chapters, we will learn a great deal about how God himself sees the church, the organization. Here, he gives us a view of the complete picture of Christendom with the input of Christ himself. No need to guess or hypothesize how the Lord sees the church; we will simply read it.

The book of Revelation opens with a greeting to the seven churches. In chapters 2 and three, we see letters written to these seven churches. These seven churches are organizations—buildings filled with believers and nonbelievers alike fellowshipping together and all claiming to be Christians. Most of them are, based on the text.

There are four layers of interpretation to these letters; all four are valid and accurate. The first and most obvious interpretation is literal. We must always begin with the literal interpretations of the Scriptures. These seven churches were literal churches placed within the cities that carried their name, or rather, the church carried the name of the city in which it resided. These seven churches each had a letter written to them from John that contained important information regarding their functioning and good and bad works. Also, God, through John, gave tips on improvement and what he wanted to see in their church, rewards he would give them, and punishments they could expect if they didn't repent of their difficulties. John wrote a letter to each of these churches and made copies of these letters so that each church received every letter. No point in reinventing the wheel. I'm sure God wanted them all to watch out for the pitfalls of the other churches as well as learning from their own mistakes. So each church received seven letters, one specifically addressing their church's problems.

In addition to the above literal interpretation, these letters also have a prophetic historical interpretation. The letters placed in the order in which God told John to put them in Revelation create a chronological history of the mainstream church. So the first letter's pros and cons actually reveal the pros and cons of the first churches; it was progressing through the persecuted church (Christians fed to the lions), through the compromised church, the Catholic church, the reformed church, etc., all the way to the end-times left-behind church of mostly unbelievers that will still be on earth during the tribulation period. This is the history of the organized church as a unit or organization. The organism "the church" made up of only believers will be raptured at the beginning of the tribulation, and we will see that as we study these churches. But there will be an organization of religious people left behind that are unsaved at the beginning of the tribulation. This chronology is profound because had John placed the letters in any other order, it would not have been accurate in this prophetic interpretation. As it is, the condition of each of these churches matches with the condition of the organized churches throughout history, and in order.

The third method of interpreting these letters is also valid and bears consideration. Each of these churches is a type of church that we see in existence today, somewhere, often in our own backyards. An honest analysis of our own church in comparison to these churches can help us avoid and correct pitfalls. An honest and critical analysis of our organization takes humility but is just as important for our church's spiritual health as it is for our own personal spiritual health. With so many church splits in our churches, we are often afraid to disagree with anything taught or run by the church. Or we are the type to criticize every little thing, majoring in the minors. Neither approach is healthy, balanced, or honest. Allowing false doctrine to be taught in the church, especially unchallenged, corrupts the church and is the true cause of church splits. On the other hand, being critical of every little minor detail that is not seen through the eyes of God and the Bible indicates control issues on our part. We are not supposed to control the direction of the church but rather surrender that control to God, not surrender that control to heretical teachers, or even to other controlling people, but to God. Finding that balance is a lifelong journey. When others make mistakes, as do we ourselves, be sure to grant them grace and honesty.

The last way we will interpret these churches is to recognize that the traits within these letters apply to us as individuals. Each letter ends with a phrase, "He that hath an ear, let him hear what the spirit says to the churches." That's me. That's you. These letters are written to the churches, not the unsaved. They are written to you and me. In the process of analyses, I must be honest and contemplate my own standing and behavior. Which church am I? Am I lukewarm? Do I work hard at working? Do I allow false doctrine in myself? Is Christ still standing outside of my life asking to be invited in? Again, humility and honesty is paramount to spiritual growth, and it's not easy.

Church of Ephesus
(Revelation 2:1–7)

Literal versus historical. Clearly it is Christ who is speaking to the church. It is originally written to a church located in the city of Ephesus. One of the meanings of the name Ephesus is "resting" or "relaxed." Wow! That's how God saw this church. They worked hard but only on physical works, not spiritual works. From a historical perspective, this is the early church. They were given the great commission, told to go out into all the world and preach the gospel, but they didn't do it. Acts tells us they stayed in Jerusalem awaiting the Lord's return. This first church was resting and waiting, not going out recruiting for the kingdom of God. They did works in their community, but they weren't supposed to be in their community.

Type of church and type of Christian

Condition. This is a good church, right? Historically, they knew Christ personally. Regardless of the interpretation, many good things are said about this church.

Positive things being said about the church are the following:

- They labor
- Have patience
- Do works
- Labor for my name
- Hate evil
- Work for Christ's name
- Test preachers and find the liars (false doctrine)
- Hate the deeds of the Nicolaitans

That's quite a string of good deeds. Lots of works and laboring. Quite the busy church. They even tested the preachers, something I rarely see done in churches today. The deeds of the Nicolaitans is a doctrine where the leaders had power over the laity (the people). This church hated this doctrine, and God hates this doctrine; our pastor is to be our servant, not wield power and authority over us. God doesn't want a person to rule over us; he wants to rule over us. He never tells the leaders of the church to take over his job, or the job of the Holy Spirit, to convict and cause our growth. He wants that job. We are to sow the seed and water; it's God who wants to cause the growth. This church held to these principles. This sounds like a good church. (Do you hear the "but" coming?)

But they lost their first love. They lost the passion and zeal that they felt when they were saved. These people were *at* Pentecost; they were physically present when the Holy Spirit first came down upon them, and they saw miracles. At that moment, they were on fire. Somehow, it's turned into a slowly burning coal. Do you know churches like this? A church that began for great reason and purpose; the people were so excited to reach out to the community. They maybe started with the intention to be welcoming to druggies and addicts, miscreants that felt uncomfortable in other churches. With all of the greatest intentions, they began prison ministries and street preaching. Years later, the same church has members that turn their nose up at the tattooed biker who stumbles in the door, still drunk from the night before; the church holds Bible studies, but nobody in the community knows about these studies or when they are so they can't participate even if they want to. There's no advertising, except from the pulpit on Sunday. Often, nobody comes anyway except to Sunday services. Many people in the community don't even know who attends the church because the members don't actively share. They've lost their enthusiasm, their vision, their first love. It becomes a love of the organization, if that.

How about you? Do you remember the hunger and zest you had at the moment of your salvation? I do. I came from a messed-up home. Loose morals, poor examples, a lot of neglect and instability. When I got saved at the age of sixteen, I was thrilled, eager to share with others, even my atheist mother. I invited Mormon missionaries and Jehovah's Witnesses into my home and discussed the issues. I studied hard and learned everything I could so I could be a better witness—a more effective witness. I spoke to strangers and passed out tracts. Even harder but with just as much enthusiasm, I witnessed at school. I shared my experience with my non-Christian friends, my teachers. I got in spats with the Biology teachers over evolution even though I didn't yet know all of the science behind creation. I fought to start a Bible study in our school during lunch time, frequented many adult Bible studies at church, and rarely missed a Sunday. Christ was my first love. He had saved me from hell but also from sadness, depression, loneliness, and an uncertain future. He had provided me with unconditional love, stability, encouragement, a guaranteed future, hope, and a definite set of morals that I could understand and count on. I wanted to share that with others.

What causes us to lose this first love? Why do we get stagnant, like a stinky old smelly pond full of algae and weeds, when we should be a raging river, loud and powerful? Well, as usual, the Bible tells if we would just read it. He tells the church of Ephesus that the solution to their problem is to remember where they came from. The opposite, then, is what caused the problem. They forgot where they came from. They got so comfortable in the pew; they forgot the crap they used to sit in. They forgot the filth God dragged them from and grew so content in their security; they forgot what it felt like sitting in the pigpen. They lost the need to drag others out of the pen with them because they themselves were no longer in the filth. He tells them to remember where they came from.

We need to take time on a regular basis remembering where we came from. We need to see others in the muck and the mire and feel how we felt when we were there. This should give us a desire to help pull them out, compassion. What if my friend from high school hadn't invited me to that tent revival? Would I have gotten into drugs, like my sister? Ended up an alcoholic like so many family members? Would I have gotten abortions, like my sister? Married multiple times, like both of my parents? Married a man who was unstable, couldn't hold a job, beat my kids? Without God, how would I have known a good man from a bad one? I certainly had no example in my own life of good men, good husbands. Without God, I had no moral compass, no vision of what my life could be like. Am I leaving others in this same ocean of hopelessness? God, I pray not.

Repent or else

God gives them an ultimatum. He tells them, and us, that we better remember where we came from, or he will remove our lampstand. What does that mean? What was the lampstand at the time that this was written? It was a cup filled with oil and had a reflector in the back that reflected the light into the room. Does this sound familiar? Our cup runneth over with the Holy Spirit. The Holy Spirit is represented in the Bible as the oil, Christ as the light (John 9:5). At the moment of my salvation, I am filled with the Holy Spirit and told to reflect Christ's love. That light is supposed to light the world, and I am supposed to let that light shine, not hide it under a bushel. This is symbolic of our witness. If I can't remember where I came from, I am no witness to others around me.

Wow, so often, we are taught that it is our works that make us a good witness. This church had a ton of works. They labored and worked; they even labored and worked for Christ's name. But in spite of these works, they had no witness. Do we so thoroughly forget what it was like to be a non-Christian that we don't even know what draws them to Christ? Trust me. Nobody says, "I have never seen Sally buy beer or wine. I want to be just like that." or "Sally has never said a cussword; now, I want to become a Christian." That's not what drew me, and I'll bet it isn't what drew you either. After all, I can be a non-Christian and choose to not buy beer or say a cussword. I can mimic moral behavior without a moral imperative. As a non-Christian, I didn't look at Sally and say, "Wow, she does so much for her church. I'm gonna become a Christian too." No, what I said was, "Wow, Christ, the son of the living God, loved me so much that he voluntarily laid down his life to save me from the consequences of my sin and provide me with a way to commune with him and spend an eternity in his presence?" Who in their right mind would turn down a gift like that? It was the light that drew me to Christ, not their work. Works produce pride; the light of Christ produces humility. When I start thinking that what *I do* reaches others, it becomes a pride trip.

It's all about Christ and his love, not about me. If I want to share my first love, I should be pointing them to Christ, encouraging them to look up to him. Our righteousness is filth before *and* after salvation. His righteousness will never let us, or others, down. All else is hypocrisy (Galatians 3:3).

Church of Smyrna
(Revelation 2:8–11)

Literal versus historical. You will notice that every letter to a church begins by describing the author. That author is never John just as the authors who wrote the Bible are not the prophets, etc. The author is Jesus Christ. The description of Christ is distinct in every letter. This church was located in a town named Smyrna which means "death." This town was named before the church, yet the name of the town and church is prophetic to the next time period in the history of the church. This church represents the persecuted church. The church began to suffer terrible persecutions all the way to the point of Christians being fed to the lions in the Roman Colosseum. This persecution forced the church to disperse and, in the process, spread the gospel.

Type of church and type of Christian

Condition. Let's see if this is a good church.
Positives things being said are the following:

- Endured tribulation and trials
- Poverty
- Suffered persecution from legalists
- Satan throws some in prison
- Faithful to death
- Hates replacement theology
- No fear

The positives listed are interesting. You will notice that the works listed are spiritual works, not physical works. This church was no doubt doing things to help others, but the works listed are things that the church had no control over. They weren't trying to rely on themselves or their righteousness. Their faith lay solely on God even in the face of death. Nothing purifies the church like persecution from the outside. Basically, if the church is suffering persecution, the tares won't grow there. If you aren't a serious Christian, why would you risk being fed to the lions for your faith? The "nominal" Christians simply admit that they are not Christians to save their own hides. This leaves the church spiritually strong, and many get saved through this dedication. This seems like a contradiction; after all, why would I want to become a Christian in the face of such danger? It's only a contradiction because we are used to seeing the physical, not the spiritual. There is no doubt, no confusion in this church. They *know* they are saved, and they *know* where it comes from.

Persecution also purifies *us*. Persecution forces us to analyze what we believe and why. Being challenged forces us to make a stand. This makes us stronger and keeps our priorities straight. It also keeps our focus off of us and on Christ. Too much focus on works becomes an ego trip and becomes pride. Instead, we should be focused on what God has done for us. This really comes about in the midst of persecution.

But repent. No buts in this church. This is one of two churches where nothing negative is said about it. God has no criticism for this church. I don't want to be a persecuted church, if I got to pick, but I sure would like God to see me in such a positive light.

Reward. Rather than being told to repent, since God says nothing negative about them, they are offered a reward for persevering. They are promised the crown of life—the crown offered to those persecuted and martyred (Revelation 2:10). There are five crowns offered for rewards in the New Testament, and this is one of them. The others are the crown of glory for serving (1 Peter 5:4), the crown of rejoicing for winning others to Christ (1 Thessalonians 2:19), the crown of righteousness for looking for his return (1 Timothy 4:8), and the crown incorruptible for living a good, healthy life (1 Corinthians 1:24–25).

Church of Pergamos (Revelation 2:12–17)

Literal versus historical interpretation. This literal church was located in the town called Pergamos which means "perverted marriage." The problems that this literal church had are the same that the historical church had in it's next stage.

After the Christians were regularly persecuted by, first, the Jews, then the Romans, Emperor Constantine noticed that the church was growing by leaps and bounds. He determined that the persecution was only strengthening the church, so he issued the edict of toleration, decreeing that the Christians would to be tolerated.

After Constantine, the Emperor Theodosius issued a decree that all must be converted to Christianity. This weakened the church since you cannot make people believe, so most faked it and just went to the "right" building to worship. Since they were not true believers, they brought their paganism with them.

Basically, they married their paganism to Christianity which is a perverted marriage—the very name of the literal city and church that John wrote the original letter to. Amazing. This was the beginning of the Catholic Church and explains many of the more pagan aspects of the church. Those members who worshipped goddesses originally brought their goddess worship with them into the church and put Mary up on a pedestal. Those that worshipped nature brought the Christmas tree and the Yule log with them. They even meshed the birth of Christ with the festival of lights which is why we celebrate our Lord's birth in December when he was actually born in the fall, probably September. Pagans who worshipped many gods changed the church and made it acceptable to pray to the many saints. Those that worshipped idols decided that they needed statues of these throughout the church to whom they would bow and pray. Those that worshipped the goddess Ishtar, the fertility goddess, meshed their beliefs with the resurrection and created the holiday Easter which celebrates the resurrection of Jesus Christ with fertility symbols like bunnies and eggs.

Mandating any religion weakens it from the inside out just as outside persecution strengthens it. The trouble then comes from the inside since you have a mix of believers and unbelievers in the same building, some wanting the truth, others bringing in false doctrine.

Type of church and type of believer

Condition._Let's see if this is a good church.
Positive things being said are the following:

- Works
- Hold my name
- Don't deny my faith
- Living in a pagan environment

The positive things spoken of show some things that God honors. He recognizes that they have the added challenge of living in a pagan environment, and that makes it harder to stay pure and strong. He sees that they do good works, that they call themselves Christian, identifying themselves with Christ. They don't deny his faith, so they recognize that Christ is the way.

Many people in our own churches call themselves Christian and hold his name. Sometimes, we rely on works as a means to get to God, and certainly, we live in a pagan environment. This means that we must struggle to keep the philosophies of the World out of our churches; don't let the current cultural views be married into your Christianity.

But God has several criticisms of this church.

- They distorted the Scripture.
- They have the doctrine of the Nicolaitans.
- They hold the doctrine of Balaam.

First, they distorted the Scripture. Although God understood the struggle that the church had being placed in a pagan environment, he does not excuse them for the choices they made within this environment. To alter or compromise doctrine or religious views to become more politically correct, or be accepted into mainstream philosophy, is another example of a perverted marriage. God recognizes the additional struggle that we have because of the society in which we live, and if we don't also recognize that, we could be fooled into the same trap the church of Pergamos was. God condemns this tactic of distorting the Scripture. The Word of God is holy, and we are told in the book of Psalm that it is even held in a higher position than his name (Psalm 138:2). He does not take kindly to our distorting it.

The doctrine of the Nicolaitans held some people in authority above others. God says that he hates this doctrine. We flirt with this false doctrine when we hold our pastors and elders up on a pedestal or when the leaders exercise authority over their fellow church members. God wants to be the authority over us, and he doesn't need men to do his job. In fact, he hates it when we try to displace his authority.

The next false doctrine mentioned is the doctrine of Balaam. This doctrine uses sin as a gateway to introduce apostasy. Wanting sin to be accepted into the church or changing your doctrine or religious beliefs to justify your sin is the doctrine of Balaam. For example, changing the doctrine of the church and marrying gays in the church and justifying their behavior as okay would be an example of the doctrine of Balaam. Loving and accepting the gay person is what Christ would have us do, but we cannot change the doctrine of the church to accept sinful behavior as not sinful. We must not lose sight of our search for the truth. Nothing, not justification of our sin, not the pagan environment around us, nothing should stand between us and our search for the truth.

Repent or else. They are told that if they don't repent of their false doctrine, then Christ will come to them with a sword out of his mouth. The sword of truth is the Word of God, and their false doctrine all began with them distorting the Word of God. Now, they will be confronted with the sword of truth—the undistorted Scriptures. This confrontation will not be pretty, I suspect. A sword is hardly a symbol of gentle correction but rather a slicing and dicing and cleansing—a painful and difficult pruning. If God uses his pure Word to measure against what we believe, uses the Bible only, how will we measure up? Do *we* measure our beliefs and the teachings of others against the Bible with honesty and humility? Or are we perverting the Scripture by marrying it to our preconceived notions and pet doctrines? Are we tolerating false doctrines to creep into our church and into our lives?

Reward. If we repent of our false doctrine, again, which began with a distortion of God's Word, then he will give us the rewards listed. The first one is the new name that he gives us. This means that those who are involved in the above false doctrines and don't repent of it will not have a new name. The implication seems to be that those that repent will be a new creature, those who don't won't be. That means those in the church that don't repent of their false doctrine may not be saved. Those who repent will also receive hidden manna. Manna is bread from heaven, and Christ is the bread of life and certainly from heaven. I know nothing satisfies the hunger of the soul like the true Bread of Life.

Church of Thyatira
(Revelation 2:18–29)

Literal versus historical. The church of Thyatira was located in the city of the same name. The name of this town means "continual sacrifice." The historical perspective coincides with the next period of the church's history which coincides with the time period of the Roman Catholic Church. The previous decree of the emperor which caused so much paganism to infiltrate the church as well as the church being mandated led to this very powerful church; this is a church that taught that communion was literally the blood and flesh of Christ, and thus, every time you engaged in the sacrament, Christ was sacrificed again. The name of the town is, once again, prophetic of the period of the church's history in order.

Type of church and type of believer

What is the condition of this church, and how does it pertain to us?

Positives

- Works (mentioned twice)
- Charity
- Service
- Faith
- Patience

These positives definitely describe what appears to be a very good church, from our perspective anyway. God gives them credit for many types of good works. He mentions works twice, charity, which is love in action, service which is another type of work, faith, and patience. This all sounds very good. It sounds like something I would want to emulate. This certainly describes that Catholic Church, as a type, but many others as well. They do many good things for many people, and that's good.

But some pretty serious negatives are listed.

- You allow Jezebel to teach my children sin and false doctrine (the doctrine of Jezebel).
- Idolatry in the church.
- Continually sacrificing what Christ ended.

The doctrine of Jezebel was the false doctrine that, again, meshed paganism with the church. It also encouraged sin to change the doctrine of the church. This is all about false doctrine, not a sinful woman. This letter specifically calls it a doctrine. Now, we simply look to the Old Testament and find the story of the woman Jezebel and study what she taught as doctrine. It is far more deceptive and subtle to mesh the truth with a lie than it is to try to sell a full-out lie. This is a common tactic of Satan's.

He continues to chew them out for idolatry within the church. We see this not only in the Catholic Church, as some would say, but also in any church that elevates anything or anyone above God. If the foundation of the church is a prophet, or the foundation of your personal beliefs is a prophet, then you need to take a serious look at this. The foundation should be none other than God and Jesus Christ.

The continual sacrifice is very serious. The belief that Christ is being sacrificed repeatedly is a direct contradiction of Scripture; Paul tells us that it was done once and for all. He tells us in Galatians that if we insist on going back into the Law, rules and requiring works, then we have made the death of Christ in vain. We do not have to continue in any type of ritual; we are free. Now our relationship with God can be mended, once and for all, through the process of regeneration. All we have to do is confess our sins and ask Christ to be the Lord of our life. Oh, and we must believe in the resurrection of our Lord and Savior. This is what God wants: a viable relationship with us, not ritual and legalism.

Repent or else the following would happen:

o   You will be given over to your sin.
o   You will be cast into the Great Tribulation that comes to the whole world.
o   Your children will be killed.

Many of these people are not even saved. Their false doctrine has prevented the truth from being taught in their church, and they have not even made Christ a true part of their lives. He is not their Lord. If they were saved, God would not give them over to their sin; the true believer is not judged on their sin, for the righteousness of Christ is imputed to them. Also, they are told they will be cast into the Great Tribulation. This is the seven-year tribulation period mentioned in Daniel, and all over in Revelation, and many more places. All Christians will be raptured at the beginning of the tribulation period, but these people will not if they don't repent.

Reward. If they repent, then he will give them Christ. *Wow!* They are a church filled with wonderful works but don't even have Christ. They can only have him if they repent. This confirms that many, if not most, of them are not saved.

Are we trying to mesh humanism, evolution, relativism, New Age movement, or other worldly views with your Christianity? Is a politically correct perspective becoming more important to us than a godly perspective? These things may become our idols if we are not careful. Are we watering down the *gospel* to please others or adding rules that require Christ's crucifixion over and over? Legalism can be dangerous to our walk and can actually prevent others from being saved. It makes the death of Christ in vain. I don't know about you, but I want no part in that.

Sardis
Revelation 3:1–6

Literal versus historical. Sardis means "escaped ones" and represents the period of the church called the reformation period. This historical period is when many escaped the Catholic Church, beginning with Martin Luther placing his thesis on the door of the church. Although we Romanticize this era in church history because it began a time when people were beginning to fight for religious freedom and trying to escape the corrupt and overbearing, oppressive rule of the Catholic Church at the time, many of these groups were just as harsh and overbearing as the church they left. John Calvin burned many at the stake for disagreeing with his religious views, and Europe and the US had periods of witch hunts whereby innocent people were tortured and killed, supposedly in the name of Christ. Even the pilgrims that came to America on the famous *Mayflower* did not believe in freedom of religion, and if you disagreed with them, they would set you out of their village and exile you to a likely death alone in the wilderness.

Types of churches and people

Condition of the church. Was this a good church?

Positives. None! God does not credit them with one positive work. He tells them, "You have a name that you live by, but you are dead." They live by the name of Christ; they claim to be Christians. They claimed (in the historical time period) to be torturing and killing them for the glory of God, but in reality, they are dead. They are not saved. I definitely want to learn from this church because I don't want to be this church!

Negatives. Now, on top of getting no compliments, they still get a butt chewing. You are dead, and *not* waiting for my return, there are a few of you who walk in Christ's righteousness.

So the vast majority are dead and not waiting for the return of Christ. People ask me all the time, "What is the advantage of waiting anxiously for the Lord's return when they have been waiting for two thousand years, and he hasn't shown up yet?" Well, here's a good reason: I don't want to be told that I am dead and not waiting for his return. There are many other reasons, but this one ought to be enough. I think one important aspect of this philosophy is as follows:

- I am deeply in love with my Lord.
- I am betrothed to him.
- My sun rises and sets on him.
- He is everything to me.

Why would I *not* be awaiting anxiously for him to be forever beside me, literally and forever. Not just spiritually but physically standing beside me so I can look at him and admire him and love him right there with me? What kind of fiancé who is madly in love with her betrothed doesn't want to see him face-to-face, isn't excited about their wedding day, and doesn't look forward to spending the rest of their life standing beside their loved one? If you are not looking for your Lord's return, perhaps you should spend a little time looking into your heart. Instead of asking me why I am waiting his return, you should find out why you are not.

Within this organization that has almost no believers in it, he does point out that there are a few within the walls that are saved.

Repent or else you won't be saved. You will not be able to inherit with the Lord because you will go to eternity in your filthy unsaved status.

Reward. *If* you repent, I will confess your name clothed in white. They are given no other reward than the right to be saved if they repent. We must all repent to receive that reward and become saved, but I think there is much more he expects of us than just our initial salvation. This church is such a mess that he is aiming them to the bear minimum—a salvation experience.

Just because you attend a church and call yourself a Christian doesn't make it so. We must make Christ our Lord and Savior and believe in our heart that God has raised him from the dead. If Christ is our Lord, then all that I am is belonging to him. He owns my heart, my body, my soul. He owns my money, my children, my property, my time. I am loyal to him and all that he asks me. I defend him, love him, and take pride in him. I am not ashamed of him. He is my Lord! I await anxiously for his return! I want to do more than escape a bad doctrine. I want to find the truth and have a relationship with God. I don't want to be this church. Only two churches have nothing good said about them, and this is the first one. I do not want to fit into the model of this church.

Church of Philadelphia
Revelation 3:7–13

Literal versus historical. Philadelphia means "brotherly love," and this is the second church where God says nothing negative about them. This was at the time John wrote the letters—an organized building filled with believers. This is the period in church history, in a timeline, that we are currently in. This is the raptured church, but before you get too lax, remember that the churches are also a type of church and a type of believer. Whether this church is you or me, specifically, remains to be seen. That's why we are studying them. Also, as a type, all of the churches coexist at the same time. Historically, this is our church though.

Type of church and type of believer

Let's check the condition of this church.

Positives

- No man shuts the door I opened.
- Have little strength.
- Kept my word.
- Not denied my name.
- Kept the word of my patience.

This is a very interesting list. The first thing that I notice is that they are all spiritual works; none of them are "works" or "deeds."

Does that mean that this church has no works? Of course not. But God has listed spiritual works, two of which have to do with his Word. This group of people are focused on the spiritual, not the physical, and they hold God's Word in very high esteem. They don't rely on their own works or strength; in fact, God congratulates them for having little strength. Does this mean they were weak? No, it means they were humble and relied on the strength of the Lord, not their own. This makes them far stronger since God's strength is much greater than my own.

Do we follow the leading of God, accepting it and walking through doors he's opened? Or do we close them because they don't fit our schedule? Do we rely on God's strength knowing that we can't do it? Or do we insist on being independent? The one to make the decisions? The one to maintain control?

Do we hold God's Word as truth? Out of five compliments, two of them pertain to his Word. Do we ignore the parts of God's Word that we don't like? Compromise by skipping parts? Refuse to balance all of it against itself? Do we like to invent our own interpretations based on what we want to hear and believe? Or do we search the Scriptures diligently looking to the Bible for the answers?

How about standing on his name? Do we get embarrassed in some company to let people know that we are Christians? Do we compromise our faith to be more accepted by our colleagues, friends, or family? Do we worry about repercussions at work, or do we stand and trust in him?

Negatives. No negatives are mentioned. God has no "but" for this church. There are only two churches that this can be said of.

Rewards. He doesn't call them to repent because they have no negatives. Instead, God intends to reap rewards on their heads.

- Those who tried to put you into bondage will worship at your feet.
- Won't go through the worldwide tribulation
- Receive crowns
- God will write his name upon them.
- New Jerusalem will be your city.

This is the church that I desire to be. I want God to look at me and only see himself. I want to please him and make him proud of me, but I can't do that through anything I do. I have to surrender to him and make it all about him if I want him to see himself when he looks down upon me. And look at the rewards. This church refused to be romanced by a works trip, and as a reward, God makes those that tried to trap them into the bondage of works bow down at their feet. The proud have become the humble. The humble have been lifted up.

He then tells them that they won't go through the worldwide tribulation. This is one of many indications of a pre-tribulation rapture. There are only two worldwide tribulations in the scripture: one is Noah's flood, the other is the seven-year tribulation also known as "time of Jacob's trouble." It's a little late for Noah's flood. And God promises this church that they will not go through the seven-year-tribulation, indicating the rapture.

He goes on to promise them crowns. There are five crowns mentioned as rewards to Christians (1 Peter 5:4; 2 Timothy 4:8; 1 Corinthians 1:24–25; Revelation 3:11, 2:10; 1 Thessalonians 2:19). Crowns are never mentioned as rewards for Israel because the Jews are not looking to be kings but rather waiting to be ruled by the King. We, however, as born-again believers will be the bride of Christ, a co-ruler, the queen, if you will. We are called kings and priests in Revelation. We see what we will do with these crowns in Revelation chapter 4. We will cast the crowns at the feet of Jesus declaring him the only one who is worthy. I want to have a crown to cast at his feet because he is worthy of them all. I want that gift to give him.

Church of Laodicea
Revelation 3:14–22

Historical versus literal. The name of this church means "rule of the people." This church has the people in control of the church. The leadership of the church makes the rules of the church and enforces them according to the set of rules they have put down. They are in control of the entire situation. Historically, this is the end-times apostate—left behind church. I don't want to be this church!

Type of church and type of believer

What is the condition of this church? Is it a good church?

Positives. None. God does not give one compliment to this church. There are only two churches that are in this condition.

Negatives. God really comes down on this church

- Apathetic (lukewarm, not hot or cold).
- Arrogant.
- Proud.
- Lacking humility.
- Christ is on the outside of the church knocking on the door.

These people don't even have Christ in the church. They don't need him. They are in control and running the church the way they see fit. They are filled with pride and arrogance and refuse to humble themselves to God and his Word.

It all begins with their apathy. They don't care. They have no passion to know the truth, no interest in learning or searching. They simply don't care one way or the other. They are the ultimate "pan triber." This is a common approach that I hear more and more in the churches today. If you try to get into a discussion of end-times, someone will invariably tell me that they have it all figured out (pride). They are not a pre-triber, post-triber, or mid-triber. They are a pantriber. It will all pan out in the end. In other words, it doesn't matter. They know nothing about it and have no interest in learning or discussing it. To them, God put all of those scriptures in the Bible, but it doesn't matter. Under the guise of saying that God will take care of it, what I'm really saying is that I don't care enough to study or learn about it. It doesn't matter.

This is apathy. It begins with relativism—a false doctrine of the world that's creeping into the church. We start out thinking that everything is relative, even truth. Our interpretation is unique to each individual. It doesn't matter what the author meant, so there's no need to try to learn what he meant. Instead, we just need to decide what the Scriptures mean to us, not to him. Well, if we believe there is no absolute truth or answers, then there is no point in searching for them. They simply don't matter. All that matters is what I want to believe. This apathy then leads to pride left and right. Now, I am the one who defines right and wrong. I am the one who recreates God into my own image. Now he must be who I want him to be, and that is different for everyone. Now, we have many gods, and we are now pagans and not believers at all! This is a very dangerous road to travel. Stay away from it!

Repent or else I will spew you out of my mouth. If they don't repent, God will have nothing to do with them. These people are not saved.

Reward. He tells them how to repent. He tells them to open the door and let Christ in. This is the salvation experience. He wants them to let him into their church and into their heart. Then the reward will be that he will commune with them, and they can sit with him on his throne. They will then be Christians. This is the promise given to every Christian, but we must first let him in!

Does your church lack interest in things spiritual? Do they study the entire Bible? How about you? Do you desire to learn the Word of God? Or do you always make excuses about other things that are more important? Do you truly want to know what it says, what it means? Who God is? Or do you only want to reaffirm what you already believe? Do you think you already have enough of it figured out? Or do you search the Scriptures diligently to see if your beliefs line up with the Word?

Are you certain, no matter what others say, no matter what verses and scriptures are presented that "it's all good?" You don't feel that it's necessary to learn more? Do you just not care enough to seek? Do you excuse your lack of knowledge and lack of interest? Trust me, we do *not* want to be this church! I, for one, do *not* want to be spewed out of the mouth of God.

Conclusion

Many of these churches do many good works but still do not measure up to God. They are not the spotless virgin that we are called to be. There are some interesting patterns that we see when we look at the churches all together.

First, there are two churches that nothing good is said about them. I want to learn from them what not to do; better understand what displeases God. Sometimes, we think we are pleasing him, but our standards and viewpoints are not his. Only through biblical example can we learn how he sees things. The two churches who graded the lowest are the church of Sardis and the church of Laodicea. In both of these churches, he indicates that the bulk of the members are not saved. To Sardis he says, "You are dead and not waiting for my return." To Laodicea, he lets them know they are lukewarm and proud, and Christ is outside the church and tells them to let him in so they can commune. The people in these two churches are not saved. This lets us know that God does not consider us to be saved by our attendance or belonging to a "club" known as a church. He does not want us to be ruled by our church but rather by him.

Next, we should look at the other two types of churches. There are three "groups" of churches. The first are the two churches where nothing positive is said: the church of Sardis and Laodicea. Now, we will look at the other two groups. One group is made up of three churches, Ephesus, Pergamos, and Thyatira. These three churches have something good said about them followed by a big "but" and "repent." The last type of church has nothing negative said about them. These churches are the model that we want to pursue. The first thing that I notice is that the positives that God mentions are of a completely different nature than the compliments he gives the other three churches. The three churches with mixed reviews have many good works mentioned to them. All of the works listed are works that are visible by their fellow man. These are all good things that we want God to be proud of us about. Some of these churches were credited for getting rid of false doctrine and testing their preachers as well as other works. We know that God wants us to put our faith into motion, which is works. And clearly, he is pleased by these churches' works. The question is, What type of works is the most desired by him? We will compare these churches' works with the churches who got an "*A*."

The churches with the highest standing have a different type of "works" listed. God has complimented their spiritual works, not their physical works. He complimented them for having no fear. They are complimented for their poverty, lack of strength, suffering, keeping the Word of God. These are all spiritual focuses, not focusing on the works that they do. There is no patting yourself on the back for having difficulty and tribulations thrust upon you. These spiritual works are not things in "our control" but rather they show that these people were giving control to God, where it belongs.

Does this mean that they didn't do the physical works? No, it means the churches with the "*C*" grade didn't have the spiritual works. God prizes the spiritual works above the physical works, so this should be my priority. Don't hold up your physical works up on a pedestal. If you are, perhaps that's all you have to offer God. Though these please him, they are not the most pleasing. Focus on your spiritual growth, your spiritual life, your spiritual walk. The other will take care of itself.

What do these spiritual gifts look like when compared to the churches with a "*C*" grade—the churches with the works, labors, and more works listed? The *C* church may say, "We are told to spread the gospel, so tomorrow, we will encourage each other and go out and hand out tracts." This is good, right? The church with no fear doesn't need to set a date. They witness to people around them all the time, on a daily basis, everywhere they go. God sees the good work of one church but sees the lack of fear in the other. He gives an "*A*" grade to the church that "no man shuts the door I opened" because that church is perpetually looking for opportunities to share; they are waiting for a door to be opened so they can run through it and witness. They don't need to pry open a door and create the opportunity themselves on a certain day when they have prepared ahead of time. They are always ready. That's the difference between the physical work and the spiritual work. Those focused on the spirit will actually accomplish more works than the church focused on doing things the right way. And God gives them an *A*. I realize that a *C* is an acceptable grade, but I want God to give me an "A." I want to please him to the maximum of my potential. I want to learn from the churches in Philadelphia and Smyrna; I don't want to stand before the Lord and hear him say, "You did pretty well, but…"

What problems plague our churches? Is it sin in the church? There certainly is sin in the church, but is that what God sees and is bothered by? We know that God is bothered by sin (an understatement, I realize), and we know that we are not to sin. So when God gives the big "but" to these churches, is that what it revolves around? Sounds logical. Instead of using logic, let's read the Scriptures. The criticisms God gives them are the following:

- Lost your first love and forgot where you came from
- Distort Scripture, hold some people in authority over others (in the church)
- The *false doctrine* of Balaam, Nicolaitans, and Jezebel
- Idolatry
- Continual sacrifice (Legalism can be seen here.)

If you look at this list, it is mostly false doctrine. Nothing there is in reference to the church being filled with sin.

We know these churches had sin, and we know our churches have sin. Why does God not mention this? Doesn't he care? Of course, he does, but the righteousness of Christ was *imputed* to the church, not earned by it. So God looks down, and he doesn't see our sin; rather, he sees the blood of Christ. False doctrine has far more damaging consequences to the church than sin. Our struggle with sin is a lifelong spiritual walk. False doctrine permeates the church and stops people from growing, from getting saved, from keeping their eyes on Christ. This is true of sin as well, but false doctrine leads to recreating God and, ultimately, idolatry. This is spiritual adultery and actually causes unbelief. It is the sin that cannot be forgiven without turning away from it. The blood cannot cover unbelief. This is the most serious offense based on the amount of attention God gives it in these letters.

Distorting the Scripture is also mentioned, and it leads to false doctrine. Taking the Bible seriously, literally and in its entirety, keeping to that Word, holding it in authority above all else, accepting all of it in context, studying it, rightly dividing this Word, all of this will chase our false doctrine away. The churches with an "A" include compliments about keeping the Word of God, and they had no false doctrine. That's why, because they kept God's Word, it corrects our rabbit trails. We cannot go down the wrong road for long before we find verses and examples that teach us what is wrong with our walk. If we study it, strive to understand it, and pray about it rather than skipping over the evidence of our wrong belief rather than ignoring it, then God will correct us. This is what we want! Don't settle. Don't accept, "I don't get it." Tell God that you want to get it. You desire to understand. You must have his truth. Let's be an *A* church. An *A* church has the potential to change the world, as Christ changed the world, because we would be carrying the power of Christ!

As the end-times grow closer, the organization becomes more and more like the end-times church of Laodicea, but this doesn't mean that we, as individual members of the organism, must be unduly influenced by this lukewarm organization. Within this end-times organization, we, strong and true believers, will find some persecution coming from within the church itself. This may surprise us but it shouldn't. After all, the organization that will exist during the tribulation period will be led by the Antichrist, and thus, they will be persecuting the tribulation saints from within the "church." But this condition isn't sudden, and we will see it as it gets closer. It's a painful thing to watch because it's a harsh betrayal to find yourself the butt of hostility within the church filled with people we love and trust simply because you have a strong stand on the Word of God.

But throughout it all, we know one certain thing: none of it surprises the Lord. None of it is beyond his control or his understanding. He has the strength to pull us through each struggle, each challenge. And he has the strength to lift us up for his glory, and he will help us be the *A* church if we only desire it, ask for his help, and submit to the leading of the Holy Spirit. Maintain humility (the opposite of pride) and be willing for him to change your beliefs when they are revealed as erroneous in the Scripture. Purge yourself of false doctrine by studying his Word and finding the contradictions and how they are actually a balance.

Find your passion and spread it! The Lord desires your passion and excitement for the Word of God!

CHAPTER 12

Conclusion

> In fact, though by this time you ought to be teachers, you need someone to teach you the elementary truths of God's word all over again. You need milk, not solid food! Anyone who lives on milk, being still an infant, is not acquainted with the teaching about righteousness. But solid food is for the mature, who by constant use have trained themselves to distinguish good from evil. (Hebrews 5:12–14)

This section of verses should cause us all to spend some time in prayer and meditation. Paul is chewing them out for not taking the Word seriously enough, for not digging into the meat. Rather, they want to hear the "first principles of God" yet again! Occasionally, someone will say, "Well, I don't understand why we need to split all of these hairs and try to figure out what such and such means. I mean, what does that have to do with me and my salvation?" Nothing! The salvation message is the first principles of God. Now that you are saved, it's time to grow! You may start with the milk, but at some point, your growth will be stunted if you don't learn to eat the meat!

To see what a mature relationship with the Lord looks like versus a younger relationship with the Lord, we can analyze our relationship with your parents. When you are a baby, you have no interest in your parents' feelings or life. You only care about yourself! You only care that your tummy is hungry, that your diaper is wet, or that you are tired. You don't care if your mother is also hungry or tired. You expect to be fed when you are hungry regardless of the feelings or conditions of your mother. It's all about the baby. When I'm a babe in the Lord, my primary focus is myself, perfectly normal. As a baby in the Lord, I want my needs met. I want my pastor to preach a sermon that means something to me every time regardless of what's going on in his life. I want the worship team to play the songs that I want, the style of music that I appreciate. I may even leave the church if they are not meeting my needs. It's all about the baby.

Back to our childhood...as my relationship with my father grows, I learn a little more about him, but most of what I understand about him is still things about my dad that relate to me. Are my eyes like his? Do I walk like him? When he comes home from work, is he in a good mood or a bad mood? I want to know his mood not because I cared as a kid about the specifics of his day but because I wanted to go to Johnny's house, and my dad would be more likely to say yes if he was in a good mood. Relating that to my relationship with the Lord...well, now, I'm searching the Scriptures, and I want to know how they relate to me. How does this section of scripture enhance my life? What does it mean in my opinion? What life lessons can I learn about it? I'm beginning to eat the meat in small pieces, mixed with lots of milk.

The relationship between myself and my parents truly reaches maturity when I want to understand who my parents are apart from myself. Now I'm losing the selfish aspect of the relationship, and I simply want to understand them as people. What makes my mother tick? How did my father get the way he is? What were their childhoods like? What are their hidden secrets and private thoughts? Our relationship with the Lord is no different. I'm truly digging into the meat in a mature relationship with him when I no longer ask, "What does this have to do with me?" When what I really want to know is, who is the Lord, really? On his own. What are his attributes like? What are his hidden secrets?

This requires us to look beneath the surface! Search the Scriptures diligently and pursue him ruthlessly. Strive to know him; rightly divide the Word of Truth (2 Timothy 2:15). Search for him with all of your heart, mind, and soul (Jeremiah). Don't stop; don't quit and don't keep it simple. The living Word won't let you down! It will speak to you, differently in each aspect of your growth process. Now we are getting into the meat, and we are beginning to fill out, grow some muscle, and truly be a man (or woman) of God!

I would like to complete our journey beneath the surface with a Shay parable. We will call it the parable of the two seas.

The Jordan River flows into two seas, both very different from the other. The first is the Sea of Galilee; the other is the Dead Sea. They are both fed by the same river—the river that Jesus was baptized in.

One sea is filled with life and fish; it is surrounded by fruit-bearing trees, beautiful green fields, and beauty. The water coming in flows back out to provide nourishment to others.

The other sea is surrounded by desert. Nothing lives in or around it. This one is also fed by the living water, but it does not allow it to pass through. It is contained in itself.

Do you receive then become a source to others? Are you surrounded by fruit-bearing trees? Are you in the midst of lush beauty? Or are you receiving then holding it all for yourself, not passing it onto others? Are you surrounded by death and desert, wondering why your life has no beauty?

We are given the Living Water to share with others. Don't live your life surrounded by death even though you've received life! Pass it onto others and watch your world bloom!

I want to relate this to Rahab, the harlot, in Joshua chapter 2 and the balance between James and Hebrews. James 2:25, specifically, and James 2:14–26, more generally, appear to contradict Hebrews 11, particularly verse 31 (and many other places that teach salvation is through faith and faith alone). Anytime I find an apparent contradiction, I *know* the solution is in the Scriptures somewhere else and found through more careful reading and studying.

The answer to the question asked in James 2:14 (What doth it profit, my brethren, though a man say he hath faith, and have not works? can faith save him?) is yes. Sometimes, it is taught that the answer is no, and people often think, *It just depends on your personal interpretation.* Well, Peter tells us there is no "personal interpretation" (2 Peter 1:20). So we need to look in the Scriptures for the answer to the question. The answer is found in Romans 10:9 (That if thou shalt confess with thy mouth the Lord Jesus, and shalt believe in thine heart that God hath raised him from the dead, thou shalt be saved.), and 1 Corinthians 3:15 (If any man's work shall be burned, he shall suffer loss: but he himself shall be saved; yet so as by fire.). The man in Corinthians had *no works*, but he himself was saved! James 2:16–17 talks about the lack of works in a particular person's life. Since he is talking about *faith with works versus faith without works*, we must assume that the person in verse 16 *is a person of faith.* He then provided no works to help his fellow man! The man of faith still has faith! (Nowhere in this section of Scripture is there talk of the man of no faith.) So faith without works is dead *to whom?* It's not dead to the man of faith nor is it dead to God. It is, however, dead to those watching. They cannot see my faith through my words alone. They cannot see my heart. They can only see my works.

Hebrews 11 makes it clear that the works come out of the faith. But without the works, the man in 1 Corinthians 3 is *still saved.* Without faith, however, he is not.

Back to Rahab in Joshua 2, let's look at this parable and this set of scriptures discussed above, and let's tie it all together. Her faith saved her. Had she never met the spies, she would've seen the Lord on the day of her physical destruction, but the analogy in the Scriptures is that her physical salvation is a symbol of our spiritual salvation and walk. Her faith is what prompted her to hide the spies and to talk to them and ask for mercy. They told her to hang the red cord from her window to alert the conquerors to which house mercy was to be showered upon. (Sounds a little like the blood on the doorpost letting the angel of death know which house to skip, doesn't it?) Then they told her that the family she was worried about would only be safe if she brought them into her house.

Let's say that her faith caused her to hang the cord for herself, but she did no works, did not get her family, told no one about what was about to happen. She would've been saved. But she would've been surrounded by death; she would've been the Dead Sea. Her faith would've been dead to all of her family and town, except the conquerors.

Instead, she hung the cord (faith) and then did the work. She went and spread the word of the coming judgment and the opportunity for grace, mercy, and protection from that judgment. In this way, her faith was now a testimony to those around her, and she became the source of life; she became the Sea of Galilee. Faith without works is the Dead Sea. It still has the living water going into it. It still has its roots in life, and the person who is the Dead Sea is still saved and will be forgiven the eternal consequences of sin. But they are surrounded by death and unnecessarily so. Faith *with* works, however, is a source of life to all those around you! And it's a much more pleasant environment for you as well! And how will we know who Christ's disciples are? By their "works?" No, by their *love*.

> By this shall all men know that ye are my disciples, if ye have love one to another. (John 13:35)

The works that Christ is looking for is the fruit of the Spirit.

> But the fruit of the Spirit is love, joy, peace, longsuffering, gentleness, goodness, faith, meekness, temperance: against such there is no law. (Galatians 5:22–23)

So be blessed by the grace and mercy of God, but don't be the Dead Sea! Be the Sea of Galilee—a sea that allows the Living Water to pass through to others that they too may be blessed! Spread the Word of God; share his love. Live your faith, and share your faith! Don't keep it to yourself. Our world, our family, our neighbors, our community may not have much time left, so don't walk, *run*!

ABOUT THE AUTHOR

Shay is an Idaho native who was thrilled to return home twenty years ago. A mother of three biological children and two children who came to her in their teens (who adds to their family with teenagers?). She is proud of all five of her children. She has been blessed to have been a homeschool mom for over twenty-three years. Each of her children has pursued different avenues, and each of them has excelled within their fields. Shay has also worked in the emergency room, been a preschool teacher, farmer of goats, Boy Scout leader, and founded a homeschool co-op. She is currently working in her local pharmacy/gift shop. She loves working with the public and being active in the community.

Shay taught children's Sunday school for many years and now teaches a women's bible study. She is married to a Bible scholar who challenges and motivates her and who is amazingly tolerant of Shay's proclivity to adopt and take in stray children and animals alike. Shay and her husband have a voracious appetite for the Word of God and spend hours studying together, debating the finer details, and hashing out interpretations in pursuit of God's truth. It is the Lord who holds it all together, and they pray that they convey this truth to those they come into contact with.

CPSIA information can be obtained
at www.ICGtesting.com
Printed in the USA
JSHW062058121122
33007JS00004B/12